Remarkable Businesswomen at the Beginning of the 20th Century

Inspiring True Stories of Women with Passion, Courage and Perseverance

(Series: Extraordinary Women in History, No.1)

By Emilia Fine

Table of Contents

Introduction   5

Why Read This Book?   7

Chapter 1: Success Factors for Creating and
Growing a Business   9

Chapter 2: Businesswomen born before 1900   17

Chapter 2.1: Helena Rubinstein (1872–1965)   23

Chapter 2.2: Elizabeth Arden (1881 – 1966)   46

Chapter 2.3: Madam C. J. Walker (1867–1919)   63

Chapter 2.4: Annie Malone (1869-1957)   87

Chapter 2.5: Anna Sutherland Bissell (1846-1934)   111

Chapter 2.6: Hattie Carnegie (1889-1956)   131

Conclusion   155

Introduction

The American Dream has inspired millions of immigrants to arrive in America to enjoy equal opportunities for prosperity and success through sheer determination, dedicated hard work, and the initiative to do something incredible. America's entrepreneurial climate has facilitated the rise of innumerable female entrepreneurs since the 18th century and even before that. Still, the most influential tier of American businesswomen emerged during the 19th and 20th centuries.

Today, the United States of America is home to over 12 million female-owned businesses, and the number continues to increase rapidly. The 2022 Annual Report released by the National Women's Business Council (NWBC) reveals that female entrepreneurs are substantial contributors to entrepreneurship in the United States, owning over 40% of the businesses operating on American soil.

The report further reveals that women are 3% more likely to start a new business than men. Presently, women-owned firms in the US have generated employment for over 9.4 million skilled professionals and workers.

Such glorifying statistics make all women proud and inspired, but they often overshadow the harsh realities of launching and operating a business in a male-dominated society. Societal expectations around a woman's job have changed dramatically, and gender roles continue to diminish. But women struggle to generate more profits and secure higher incomes that compete with their male counterparts' income and profitability potential.

The high disparity in wage, opportunities, and accessibility remain a grave concern. Still, as we examine the challenges faced by female entrepreneurs during the 19th and 20th centuries, we notice the significant improvements in today's entrepreneurial climate. Encouraging female entrepreneurs to rise and thrive is essential to facilitate positive social change, because women in business are much statistically more committed to giving back to their communities.

Why Read This Book?

This book seeks to inspire its readers by regaling them with mind-blowing stories of female entrepreneurs who rose from slavery and the poverty-ridden lives of immigrants arriving on the shores of a foreign land to become the sole owners and operators of multimillion-dollar businesses.

These powerful women overcame innumerable hardships and struggles, the biggest being the societal expectations of gender that governed their lives, which threatened to kill their entrepreneurial visions with the oppressive burden of domestic responsibility and religious ideals. Examining their hurdles will give readers guidance and motivation to stay committed to their goals.

This book details the stories of 6 iconic trailblazers who changed their own lives and transformed their communities, leaving behind a long list of highly-notable contributions that deeply engraved their names in the glorious pages of history. This book will inspire its readers to adopt community service as a crucial element of their roadmap to success, because we can only achieve sustainable success and growth through business models that aim to uplift us alongside our communities.

Reading this book is akin to embarking on an inspirational journey to extract the key ingredients of success, as depicted in the compelling stories of influential female historical figures. This book makes a deliberate effort to ground its readers in a moving process of contemplation, encouraging them to compare their entrepreneurial struggles with those of female leaders who achieved success at a time when America was gripped first by a fierce, evangelical fever, and later by two tumultuous world wars.

How will this comparison help? It will enable readers to grasp the factors that attract success and identify the tendencies that repel triumph and confine our progress to cyclical disappointments and failures. Reading this book will help readers renew their motivation and rekindle their passion for their dreams, fueling them with the fire of entrepreneurship and innovation.

Readers need not force themselves to read this book cover to cover; they can flip through the chapters and pick any story that deeply resonates with their ideals, values, and journey as an entrepreneur.

Chapter 1: Success Factors for Creating and Growing a Business

It has taken hundreds and thousands of years to accept the idea of women operating as independent businesspersons or partners in male-owned business enterprises. Female entrepreneurs have been overshadowed by their male counterparts throughout history, and one can find innumerable examples of this disparity even in modern-day corporate environments.

Throughout history, women's entrepreneurship has never been as significant as it is today, with a highly facilitative ecosystem that inspires and facilitates female-led business ownership with enhanced accessibility. But in the 18th and 19th centuries, women business owners overcame unprecedented challenges and insurmountable odds.

They achieved their dreams in economic, political, and social environments that pitted them against seemingly impossible challenges – and this success was only made possible by their unfaltering dedication and unwavering determination. The powerful stories of female entrepreneurs narrated in this book are extraordinary tales of preservation. All these dynamic boss ladies rose to astounding success from the bottomless pits of poverty with no formal education, but a deep-rooted yearning to learn and grow.

Women have cemented themselves as dynamic creative disruptors and ingenious innovators, managing their domestic responsibilities alongside monumental contributions to beauty, commerce, fashion, manufacturing, and trade. With their entrepreneurial acumen and community-centric vision, female entrepreneurs have compelled the world to rethink its patriarchal gender roles and create more room for female trailblazers and their boundless passions.

Each story narrated in this book carries within itself a treasure trove of lessons on overcoming hardships and staying true to one's core passion. Each story's key ingredients for success revolve around the same trajectory: a burning desire to learn and perfect one's craft, fueled by the curiosity to unravel new phenomena and the agility to test emerging possibilities.

Resilient and successful, these women possess unyielding courage and unfaltering perseverance to continue treading the same path with a willingness to alter the route without losing track of the destination. Leaders are never so disappointed or dejected that the process of self-improvement after failure is stopped; in fact, they excel at self-reflection and reinvention.

Trailblazers always keep their eyes focused on the prize, refusing to let external opinions blind them to their dreams, or social norms dissuade them from pursuing their desires. These creative minds thrive on intellectual stimulation and innovation and are constantly consumed by the need to ask questions and find answers. Instead of focusing on problems, leaders have a solutions-oriented mindset that helps overcome even the most complex challenges.

Helena Rubinstein began her journey as the daughter of a humble Polish food merchant, desperate to escape a marriage arranged by her father and carve out an independent life that would quench her thirst for success and fame. At the culmination of her journey, Helena Rubinstein was known worldwide as the woman who invented beauty – the first to introduce the idea of scientific research and development in the formulation of cosmetics and skincare products!

With her creativity, masterful branding skills, and unmatched guile, Helena entwined cosmetics with science to compel 19th-century society to change centuries-old perceptions. Back then, using makeup and skincare products was associated with prostitution and "morally corrupt" women. Helena transformed mindsets, using her relentless drive and focus on changing this view to turn the morally-questionable act of beautifying oneself into a multimillion-dollar global industry.

Helena stands out with her perseverance and courage to defy societal norms and actively campaign against them to become a harbinger of positive social change. But the most striking and profoundly-resonating success factor that one can embrace in Helena's story is her determination to continue educating herself.

Helena Rubinstein had an unquenchable thirst for knowledge and intellectual stimulation, surrounding herself with leading cosmetology, hygiene, herbal medicine, and skincare experts to become the best, most credible expert in the beauty industry. Rubinstein actively sculpted her mind and body, working hard to embody her high moral and social ideals and become the woman she aspired to be.

Her desire for continual learning and improvement paved the road for groundbreaking innovations, allowing Helena Rubinstein to emerge as a potent disruptor who discarded the old ways and introduced women to research-backed approaches to nurturing and caring for themselves.

The success story of Elizabeth Arden, famous for introducing American women to numerous makeup innovations, including eye makeup, travel-sized products, and in-store makeovers, is a riveting lesson on taking risks and persisting in the face of disastrous failures. Elizabeth Arden was a mighty force of nature, armed with matchless confidence and an unwavering dedication to her dreams.

Despite being overwhelmed by repeated failures, she refused to give up and always came back with a better, more effective strategy. Elizabeth's journey and eventual success underscore the significance of supporting one's dreams through whatever means necessary. For over two decades, Elizabeth Arden did a series of odd jobs, working as a cashier, dental assistant, secretary, and stenographer to save up enough money to fund her dream. And that's precisely what she did!

She saved $1,000 from her series of jobs, including her last stint at a beauty parlor, and used those funds to launch her beauty salon with partner Elizabeth Hubbard. Unfortunately, the partnership didn't last long, but instead of being demoralized by this failure, Elizabeth Arden stayed committed to her dream and bought her partner out rather than giving up on her business.

The story of Madam C. J. Walker, born Sarah Breedlove, radiates fierceness and power with its ability to humble and inspire those who fail to stay true to their dreams despite hailing from privileged backgrounds. Born to formerly-enslaved people, Sarah Breedlove was the first free member of her family. Her pursuit of prosperity and success liberated her and empowered her African American community.

Sarah Breedlove reinvented herself as Madam C. J. Walker – a woman who inspired hundreds and thousands to muster the willingness to work hard and be one's inspiration in achieving success. Madam Walker was carving her path toward successful entrepreneurship at a time when politics and society wanted to confine African American women to menial jobs like washing dirty linens and domestic service.

Madam Walker lit her own path to success. In the process, she set ablaze a fire that lit up everything in its wake, illuminating an entire community that had been overshadowed by white supremacy for centuries. She believed in creating and finding her own opportunities and did not seek out shortcuts to reach her destination.

Madam Walker's story inspires us to believe we all have hidden strengths we've never actualized or identified. She once said, "*I got my start by giving myself a start,*" inspiring everyone to begin their passion projects today instead of waiting for the right time.

Annie Turnbo Malone, the mentor of Madam C. J. Walker and hundreds of other African American women, inspired people to adopt a community-oriented mindset to benefit others with our own success. Annie Malone's success story reveals that, at times, reinventing yourself is the best way to eliminate roadblocks and feel inspired.

Annie was intrigued to solve the problem of finding the right hair products to nurture and strengthen the unique hair type of

African American women. She found the solution and, in the process, managed to solve a problem had that plagued women of African descent throughout America and worldwide. But Annie did not abandon her penchant for problem-solving, even after she had bottled her solutions and amassed a multimillion-dollar empire from an extensive sales and distribution network.

Instead, Annie Malone kept finding new problems and innovating solutions. She teaches us to invest in ourselves through education, self-care, and self-nurturing and collaborate with like-minded creatives who share our vision.

Above all, Annie Malone inspires us to find avenues for success that benefit our community. After educating and empowering herself, Annie used her financial independence and power to empower and uplift hundreds and thousands of African American women through her Poro College of Beauty.

Anna Sutherland Bissell, America's first female CEO, teaches us the significance of being our own boldest and loudest promoters, branding and marketing our dream projects with an aggressive energy that compels everyone to listen attentively. Anna and her husband, Melville, visited numerous cities, towns, and villages, running door-to-door campaigns until their product became a global hit, churning out millions of dollars.

Anna was a gifted and relentless problem-solver who refused to give up, even in the face of crippling adversities. Anna

Sutherland Bissell rescued her company from bankruptcy and failure after a fire had destroyed their factory, resulting in unprecedented losses and acute financial strain. Anna used her interpersonal and marketing skills to secure sizable loans from financial institutions, reinventing and transforming her business with an extensive reconstruction process.

Most importantly, Anna Sutherland Bissell's story teaches us the significance of being attuned to the needs of the people who work for us and fostering a sense of community within the workplace.

The inspiring journey of Hattie Carnegie, the style connoisseur who gave America a unique fashion identity, teaches us that success comes from dedicated effort and staying true to oneself. Like other successful women depicted in this book, Hattie Carnegie prioritized learning and professional development. She planned as many as seven yearly trips to Paris to learn from the grand fashion maestros and perfect her craft to remain on top of her game.

These influential and inspiring women teach us to invest emotionally, mentally, and physically in pursuing our dreams and chasing our passions with unwavering dedication.

Chapter 2: Businesswomen born before 1900

Economists and historians have unjustly overlooked women's contributions to the economy and society, given the inaccurate depiction of their professional records. The 1900s witnessed women from the working class participating in multiple irregular forms of labor. Many from low-income families had little choice but to step out to support their families.

Women worked in factories, offered domestic services to affluent households and nobles, ran home-based enterprises, and participated in the operations of family-owned businesses. They commonly led home-based enterprises focused on knitting and sewing, often helping factories outsource their garment and shoe-manufacturing processes. Women were also involved in food businesses and the upkeep of agricultural and livestock farms.

Despite their active involvement and far-reaching economic contribution, women's work was not recorded in labor statistics, nor were they treated as salaried employees. This lack of record-keeping and representation through labor laws altered societal perspectives on women's capabilities – regarding them as secondary workers with menial earnings.

The 19th century portrayed the man as the primary breadwinner and head of the family, with the woman trailing behind as his primary helper, domestic manager, and provider of emotional support. History reveals that women have successfully owned and operated profitable business enterprises since the dawn of society, but it has taken centuries for their work to be applauded and recognized.

In the United States, the 19th century brought the evangelical fever of the Second Great Awakening, which swept the country in a frenzy of religion-inspired gender expectations. Women were expected to fit in with the persona of an elegant, well-heeled woman with strong religious beliefs and a lace fan to accentuate her innocence. These societal stereotypes and gender roles promoted by evangelical Protestantism changed women's economic, personal, and social lives across America.

The beliefs transformed how women could participate in economic and social settings and dictated how they should feel, live, and think. Individuals with moral and religious authority began defining how women should design their lives, diminishing their traditional economic role and reducing their household production.

Women became nurturers and homemakers, and their home-based enterprises were replaced by a religiously-motivated devotion to serving their children and husbands to feel morally elevated. Many historians argue that the ideas of a "traditional home" and the woman as the "homemaker" were coined in 19th century America.

The gender roles and stereotypes of Colonial America positioned men as superior to women economically, emotionally, physically, mentally, and even morally! The 19th century bore witness to economic structures becoming heavily dominated by a patriarchal hierarchy. Patriarchy has existed for centuries, but in Colonial America, it allowed men to control political power, wealth resources, and even matters of religious beliefs.

As America was grappling with patriarchal religious dogmas and male-dominated power spheres, the Market Revolution arrived – another powerful catalyst that shifted gender roles by making economic life highly commercialized. The rapid demise of subsistence farming transformed the American way of life, and plantations were replaced with factories and textile mills. In the early 20th century, most middle-class and working-class American women were involved in "home-making" and serving their families.

Findings of the American Census Board from that period reveal that women only comprised 20% of the labor force, categorized as "gainful workers". The authorities should have recognized women's economic contributions, as many domestic chores revolved around managing the family estate or business.

The early 20th century witnessed a significant influx of African American women into the American labor force. Unlike white women, they were more likely to continue working even after getting married and having children. Interestingly, women who continued working after marriage were considered morally flawed because they defied cultural norms. Back in the day, women's education was not considered a necessity, and the education and skill-based knowledge given to them did not support a lucrative profession.

For instance, upper-class and middle-class women in America were taught how to embroider and sew, run their households, manage domestic staff, wear frilly dresses, and play the refined hostess. The career paths and opportunities available to young, ambitious women were heavily circumscribed. Women from low-income families were trained as domestic staff or piece workers doing dirty and unsafe factory jobs.

Until the 19th and early 20th centuries, businesses owned and operated by women were alehouses, brothels, hotels, inns, shops, millineries, and taverns. After losing their men, these women were forced into entrepreneurial ventures to put food on their tables. This discussion draws attention to a glaring truth: Business ownership and entrepreneurialism were not seen as ambitions or opportunities for women but rather as a path to achieve financial stability and avoid being labeled a social burden.

The 19th and 20th centuries were tumultuous periods that introduced disruptive philosophies that eventually destroyed centuries-old monarchical and patriarchal power structures. Ideologies like communism, consumerism, feminism, mass immigration, and progressivism created a conducive environment for female entrepreneurship to thrive and gain widespread acceptance.

Interestingly, most female-led business ventures from this period primarily targeted female consumers. Women entrepreneurs from this period were motivated by a defining sense of purpose rather than the economic equations of profit maximization.

The Second World War was a dramatic period with a far-reaching and multifaceted impact worldwide. Still, in the context of female entrepreneurship in America, it transformed gender roles and brought women to the forefront of economic activity. It liberated women by forcing them to take the wheel of the family finances while their husbands and breadwinning men fought the enemy on the battlefields.

The "War Time Wife" played a dynamic role in sustaining the economy. This ideal inspired women across America to start business ventures and carve their own economic identities.

This section will explore the inspiring stories of incredible women who managed to chase their passions and actualize their entrepreneurial dreams in a world riddled with adversities. These trailblazers stayed true to their visions and committed to their passions at a time when the playing field was tilted against them, pitting them against patriarchal social norms and subjugating gender roles.

Chapter 2.1: Helena Rubinstein (1872–1965)

"I worked and worked. Although days only have 24 hours, I worked 50! Imagine, not only did I prepare my creams by hand, I also put them in pots, stuck on the labels – and then sold them. I did the publicity; I went from store to store with my products. At that time, pharmacies were the only outlets. I went to six in a week, eight the next week. Luckily, I wasn't lacking for energy."

— Helena Rubinstein

The life and work of Helena Rubinstein reveal an awe-inspiring tale of determination, passion, perseverance, and strength. The story of the woman who revolutionized the beauty industry and taught women how to pamper and nurture their skin began with a simple desire to break free from ordinary life and do something magically incredible.

Helena was consumed by the desire to control her destiny and leave her mark on this world, and her ambition and dedication found the perfect outlet in her mother's homemade skincare cream. A box of cream was all Helena needed to unleash her entrepreneurial acumen and creativity, setting the foundations of a self-made career that emerged into a global beauty empire.

Helena was the first cosmetician who incorporated scientific ingredients and research to develop skincare products. She was a true pioneer whose intellect and innovation were considered way ahead of her time. In an age when women were reduced to labels like "caregiver" and "homemaker", Helena dodged an arranged marriage and embarked on a powerful journey of self-empowerment and self-discovery.

She not only discovered her true calling, but created a globally-renowned business empire that has thrived for over 120 years and continues to amass new patrons worldwide. Let's dive deep into Helena's story and unravel her adventures from Poland and Australia to the UK and the United States.

The Beginning

Born to Jewish parents, Augusta and Horace Rubinstein, in Krakow, Poland on Christmas Eve (December 24) 1870, Helena was the eldest of 8 daughters. Her father, Horace, was an unsuccessful and temperamental wholesale food broker, who was quite strict with his wife and daughters. Augusta Rubinstein, Helena's mother, was a powerful woman and breathtaking Polish beauty and one of the most inspiring role models for Helena and her sisters.

Augusta was convinced that her daughters, Helena, Pauline, Regina, Rosa, Ceska, Erna, Stella, and Manka, would become influential and powerful. She taught her daughters to aspire to more than just a husband and a home, inspiring them to harbor dreams and ambitions and gain power through their beauty and ability to love and nurture others.

Self-care was a strong notion in the Rubinstein household, and Augusta encouraged her daughters to preserve their youth and vitality by taking good care of their skin. A captivating beauty herself, Augusta spent hours pampering herself, and her friend, renowned Polish actor Helena Modjeska, would supply her with beauty tips and elixirs.

Helena Modjeska introduced Mama Rubinstein to a Hungarian chemist in Krakow, Dr. Jacob Lykusky, who created a herbal formula to brighten, moisturize and hydrate the skin. Dr. Lykusky's cream, named the Modjeska cream, was formulated with a concoction of herbs, extract of the Carpathian fir bark, and essence of cold-pressed almonds.

This beauty elixir gave Helena the medium and motivation to start her journey toward self-empowerment, serving as a potent catalyst that fueled her dreams!

Back then, concocting homemade pomades and poultices was a prevalent Polish tradition. Women created DIY recipes to protect their skin from the sun and chilly winters. Helena's family fostered a deep friendship with Dr. Lykusky, who later became "Uncle Jacob" and a pivotal contributor to Helena's skincare business.

Being the eldest of eight siblings, Helena was often responsible for the household and domestic responsibilities. Her father had no sons to help him with the family business, and Helena's mathematical acumen and book-keeping skills encouraged Horace to bring her into the family business. She presided over her first business meeting at the age of 15, covering for her father, who was ill and bedridden that day.

Based on Helena's account, her mother gave her thoughtful advice that she held onto for years to come. Augusta said, "*If you want to be clever, listen well and talk little.*"

As Horace's dying business began to thrive under Helena's dedicated entrepreneurship, Horace realized that she had the potential to do much more. He decided that Helena should pursue medical science and become a clinician. Helena was enrolled in the University of Krakow to begin her medical education. She enjoyed working in the laboratory, but the stressful nature of the day-to-day workload and the unpleasant odors of the hospital drove her to sickness.

Working in the hospital denied Helena the opportunity to unleash her entrepreneurial creativity and actualize the ambitions that were fueling her passion. She was deeply unhappy, and her body language and withdrawal from life showed this discontentment. She became frail and thin, and these changes caught her father's attention. One day, while doing her daily rounds, Helena fainted in the wards.

Her family was deeply concerned. Upon discussing the matter, Horace agreed that Helena should end her medical education – but on one condition!

He wanted Helena to get married to a 35-year-old widower – a wealthy contender for his 18-year-old daughter's hand. As determined and headstrong as she was, Helena rejected his proposal and brought out her beau, Stanislaw.

Stanislaw was a non-Jewish medical student whom Helena had met during her time at the University of Krakow. All hell broke loose at the Rubinstein household, because the idea of a young Jewish girl bringing home a non-Jewish beau was too outrageous even to comprehend, let alone agree to. This was a time when women were widely considered the property of men, from their fathers and brothers to their husbands and children.

The concepts of self-identity and freedom must have been inconceivable for women in this time. Still, trailblazers like Helena Rubinstein were non-conformists who refused to bow down to societal subjugation and focused on finding a way out of their patriarchal predicaments. Helena began planning her escape route and wrote a letter to her mother's brother, Uncle Louis, requesting that he allow her to travel to Australia and live with his family. Uncle Louis agreed, and thus began the most exciting chapter of Helena's life!

Australia – Helena's Land of Opportunity

Helena's uncle, Louis Silberfeld, lived with his wife and children in Colerain, Western Victoria. Louis worked as an oculist and store owner, supporting his family with a comfortable income. As soon as he wrote back extending an invitation for Helena to come and live with his family, the determined Rubinstein began planning her escape.

This was her best chance to take her life into her own hands and write her own story – and no one could stop her, as far as she was concerned!

Helena packed her bags and left for Australia with 12 pots of her mother's beauty elixir, the Modjeska cream. In the summer of 1894, when Helena set out on this life-changing journey, she changed her name before filling out the ship's passenger list paperwork. Born as Chaja Rubinstein, she renamed herself Helena – inspired by the beautiful and vivacious Helen of Troy. Helena also recorded her age as four years younger than she actually was.

Upon arriving in Victoria, Australia, Helena was baffled by the striking differences between the Australian and Polish ways of life, especially the way Australian women neglected their beauty and skincare. A stylish and smartly-dressed woman with soft, porcelain skin, Helena commanded awe and drew compliments wherever she went.

Some called her haughty and difficult, while others wanted to know the secret behind her youthful radiance and glowing skin. Communication was a challenge, for Helena did not speak English, and aside from her uncle's family, she couldn't communicate with anyone in Polish. So, Helena enrolled herself in a small school in Coleraine to learn the English language.

Helena would routinely shock her teachers with her openness and eagerness to ask questions that would often make the women of her time squirm and swoon in response to her forwardness. Once, she asked, *"What does 'bugger' mean? My uncle calls me that."*

Colonial Australia was less forward and open-minded than Poland, for Polish people are open and frank communicators who don't hold back or fuss over the trivialities of polite society. These changes were overwhelming for Helena, but she was actively learning to adjust and fit into her new life.

In those days, Australian women had no skincare or cosmetic product access. They scrubbed their faces and bodies with simple soap and water. Any creams, emulsifiers, or foundations were considered "the devil's instruments" and regarded with skepticism and suspicion. Women who used such concoctions were berated, their moral character was questioned, and they were branded as "the devil's helpers".

Despite these conflicts surrounding the notions of skincare and cosmetic products, Helena's flawless complexion and radiant skin tone continued to attract women in her community. Many local women with a deep understanding of the dry spells induced by the harsh Australian sun and wind implored Helena to give up the secret beauty elixir she used to maintain her complexion and suppleness.

Helena would religiously slather her skin with Dr. Jacob's herbal cream, but instead of sharing the cream or the formula with her Australian admirers, she decided to start a business!

Helena Rubinstein saw an opportunity in the Australian women's skincare qualms and decided to capitalize on it by duplicating the formula of the Modjeska cream. The recipe needed generous portions of lanolin, extracted from the sheep's wool – a key ingredient abundant across Western Australia. However, lanolin had an unpleasant and pungent odor that would discourage potential customers.

Helena decided to undermine this odor with a combination of water lilies, pine bark and lavender, resulting in a fragrant cream. She marketed this product as a concoction of rare herbs and named it "Valaze".

Valaze sold like hotcakes, and Helena emphasized her cosmetic genius and herbal talents by regaling customers with her brief enrollment in medical science.

Building an Empire

As the business started to grow, Helena relocated to Melbourne and began working on building a venue where she could sell her products. She found temporary work as a waitress and began scouting the market for an investor who could fund her star product, the *Crème Valaze*.

Interestingly, the woman who agreed to fund Helena's business, Helen MacDonald, was one of her most loyal customers and a firm believer in the product's effectiveness as it had significantly improved her complexion. Helen Macdonald invested $1,500, which allowed Helena to establish sufficient stockpiles of the cream, alongside renting and furnishing a shop.

In 1902, Helena opened her first beauty salon in the O'Connor Building at 138 Elizabeth Street, Melbourne. Named *Helena Rubinstein, Beauty Salon*, this intimate space was a labor of love for Helena. She painted the walls and sewed the curtains herself; even the store-sign was her own creation. Helena personally catered to all the women who walked into her salon, absorbing and learning everything she could about her clientele and fostering great customer relationships.

It took her some time to realize that more than one product would be needed to run an entire salon where women would come with many skincare issues. She began experimenting with herbal formulas in the kitchen to create creams for various skin tones and types. With time, Helena realized that products that work wonders weren't enough to sell skincare to women. The processes needed a special touch to draw customers in and encourage them to buy.

Therefore, she encouraged women to visit the salon and have their skin examined and diagnosed for concerns, followed by a treatment prescription. This strategy turned out to be a raving success, and within two years, Helena Rubinstein was the go-to skincare guru in Melbourne society.

Melbourne had no shortage of beauty salons, hairdressers, nail salons, and massage parlors, but Helena Rubinstein's beauty salon offered Australian women something new and empowering! Instead of selling products, Helena talked to them about their skin qualms and made them believe they could look and feel beautiful if they invested a little in caring for and pampering their skin.

Her interactions with many women facilitated first-hand training and knowledge of the various skin types. She realized that there was a need to make products tailored to three basic skin types: dry, normal, and oily, alongside three white-dominated complexions: blonde, brunette, and redhead. Helena Rubinstein was the first cosmetician to propose that each skin complexion and type needed a unique skin-nurturing solution.

Women flocked to the salon, begging Helena to help them to address common concerns like blemishes, freckles, and scars. Helena would dispense great advice, encouraging them to cleanse regularly and stay out of the sun.

As Helena's popularity spread nationwide, magazines began publishing stories of her cosmetic insight and herbal concoctions. Eugenia Stone, the editor of a countrywide women's magazine, traveled from Sydney to Melbourne to interview Helena, amassing nationwide publicity which resulted in an influx of orders from all over Australia.

Helena managed to pay off her $1,500 investment and expanded her business to Sydney. She had enough money to bring Dr. Jacob Lykusky to Melbourne and set up a facility to develop cosmetic and skincare products. According to her own admission, Helena worked 18 hours daily for over two years to maximize her profits and expand her business.

Helena's dream began materializing into a business empire, one of the world's first cosmetic brands. She started involving her family in managing the enterprise, and many of her sisters were appointed to run various aspects of the company. First, Helena invited Ceska, her third youngest sister, to help her to manage business affairs, and the rest started following soon after.

As her business grew and profits started to multiply, Helena's ambition and hunger for more quadrupled. The Australian market wasn't enough to contain and support Helena Rubinstein's passion for business, and she began setting her sights on foreign markets in Europe and beyond.

However, Helena's dreams were curtailed by the fact that women were not considered suitable candidates for business loans in the 20th century. She overcame that roadblock by saving up the money herself. She decided that adding investors or partners to her business would result in unwanted complications, and saving would be the wisest solution.

During this period, Helena met and fell in love with Edward William Titus, an American journalist of Polish descent. This distracted her from her core passion, an experience which genuinely rattled her because she had never visualized herself swooning into romance. Her work was the passion that consumed every ounce of her romantic energies, so when Edward proposed, Helena declined despite acknowledging her love for him.

She agreed to marry him after setting up a salon in London and selling her product across England. In five long years, she managed to save $100,000 – enough to open her first beauty salon in London!

The Helena Rubinstein Beauty Salon opened on Grafton Street, in the former residence of Lord Salisbury. This was a significant milestone for Helena, who realized the importance of appealing to the rich clientele and satisfying the highly-discerning British ladies with adequate know-how and training. In 1905, Helena returned to Europe and poured herself into learning and training.

She studied under the tutelage of renowned European experts, learning everything she could about facial surgeries, skin-healthy nutrition and diet, and skin treatments. In Paris, Helena Rubinstein studied with the renowned French organic chemist Dr Marcellin Berthelot. She even invited Vienna's sought-after peeling expert Dr. Emmie List to work for her in London.

In 1908, Edward Titus visited her in London and proposed again. This time, a 38-year-old Helena accepted, and the couple were married in a private ceremony. Edward was deeply involved in Helena's dreams and routinely advised her on crucial business matters. According to Helena's autobiography, Edward even created some appealing advertisements for the salon.

The same year, Helena opened a salon in Wellington, New Zealand, and her second store in London.

Becoming the Woman Who Invented Beauty

Helena Rubinstein was more than just an entrepreneur who capitalized on women's desire to beautify themselves. She was the woman who invented beauty – one of the first creative innovators who believed that beauty is every woman's prerogative, provided they invest in self-care and nurturing.

Becoming the woman who invented beauty was a long, dedicated journey into self-educating and learning from renowned experts worldwide. In 1905, Helena went to Europe to visit her family and then traveled across European capitals to educate herself on foreign beauty and skincare rituals.

In Vienna, Helena toured the local spas, which fascinated her with science-backed treatments like body wraps, chemical peels, and hydrotherapy. She consulted Vienna's renowned chemical peel expert, Dr. Emmie List, and recruited him to develop similar skincare treatments for her salon in London.

In Paris, Helena signed up for hygiene workshops from the renowned French chemist and physicist, Marcellin Berthelot, to learn about skin cleansing rituals and disinfecting the skin with bleach. Helena found chemists, dermatologists, and hygiene experts and absorbed all the knowledge they had to offer.

She learned various medically-researched techniques to diminish the appearance of fine lines and wrinkles. She studied the impact of diet and nutrition on the physical appearance of the body and skin. Helena was particularly intrigued by massage therapies and how electrical stimulation and rollers could enhance the skin's suppleness by speeding up blood circulation.

Rubinstein incorporated her knowledge into her business with masterful blends of creativity and innovation. She was the first to introduce scientific concepts and medically-researched techniques into cosmetics and skincare, helping women understand that beauty is inward out, and the skin reflects internal health.

The Helena Rubinstein Beauty Salon experience evolved dramatically, incorporating cutting-edge cosmetic and skincare techniques inspired by hygiene and skin-nurturing rituals from all over the world. Women visited the salon for skincare formulas, slimming tablets, and luxurious massages with electric body rollers. She had specialized skincare products to combat acne, fine lines, and sun damage.

But clients weren't just getting products and services from the salon – Helena was preaching a new beauty philosophy by advising her clients to combine her products with a low-fat, nutrient-rich diet, regular exercise, and proper breathing. She wanted to educate women on how to care for their bodies and skin to feel and look beautiful, encouraging them to eat plenty of fruits and vegetables and stay hydrated. As Helena would say, *"There are no ugly women, only lazy ones."*

Helena was a dedicated and determined hard worker, prioritizing continual learning to dispense practical advice to her clients. She was one of the first influential trailblazers in the beauty industry to raise awareness about the habits that benefit and harm the skin and overall health. Even her advertising and marketing campaigns raised awareness, with personalized messaging instead of the gender promoting gender roles, which was typical of advertisements from that era.

Instead of appealing to female sensibilities with superficial content, Helena published brochures and instructional manuals outlining the significance of nutritious diets and regular exercise, and dispensing valuable insight into the hazards of sun exposure. Helena once said, *"I am more than ever convinced that what we eat today is what we are tomorrow."*

She continually emphasized the importance of self-learning and identifying one's individualism. Her ideas and marketing tactics were amazingly radical for her time, and her impact on women's beauty and skincare rituals was far-reaching and enigmatic. The woman who invented beauty transformed how women took care of themselves, and by this time, her success in the cosmetic industry was undisputed and unmatched.

Expanding and Glamourising the Helena Rubinstein Brand

While Helena occupied herself with self-education and product development, Edward focused on glamourizing the brand and networking on behalf of the salons. Edward would squire her to glamorous parties across Australia and Europe, taking her to fine dining establishments, outstanding theatrical performances, and balls where she could brush shoulders with notable celebrities and affluent patrons.

Edward's charm, intellect, and quick-wittedness made him an excellent choice to manage the business's advertising and public relations aspects, and Helena delegated these duties to his skilled hands. Edward started by changing Helena's public image, instructing her to go by the title "Madame" and introducing her to trend makers and creative artists like Virginia Woolf, George Bernard Shaw, J.M Barrie, and Somerset Maugham.

It didn't take long for Edward's tactics to work, and soon, the Helena Rubinstein Beauty Salon became a popular hangout spot for the British elite and Europe's most sought-after stage actresses. Helena's friendships with European performers and actresses like Edna May, Fanny Ward, Gabrielle Ray, and Kate Cutler inspired her to develop a cosmetic line with makeup products designed for regular women.

She began including actresses and celebrities in the advertising campaigns for Valaze cream to spend more time in their company and learn how they beautified their facial features with makeup. She remembered their art of beautification, from how they used tinted facial powders to lining their lips with red pigments and darkening their eyes with kohl.

It is important to understand that in the early 20th century, middle-class and working-class women who used makeup products were considered morally questionable. These were the women that Helena Rubinstein wanted to inspire, and she understood that changing their grooming habits would be a slow and tiresome process.

In contrast, Helena's high-society clientele, like the British Prime Minister's wife, Margot Asquith, and Baroness Catherine Flame d'Erlanger, embraced the pigments and foundations, becoming regular patrons of the Maison de Beauté Valaze.

Baroness Catherine d'Erlanger, Helena's friend and patron in Parisian high society, popularly known as *"la Flemme"* for her voluminous red locks, introduced Rubinstein to a glorious world of arts. Helena and the Baroness would scout the streets of Paris for rare antiques, spending hours at flea markets and antique stores. She took Helena under her wing, introducing her to renowned artists like Jacob Epstein, honing her fascination for Baroque and Rococo art, and helping her shop for Venetian artworks and furniture.

Helena emerged as one of her period's most influential and generous art patrons, amassing a fortune's worth of prized antiques, artworks, sculptures, and furnishings.

Undisputed Success in America

In 1914, Helena and her family left Europe to escape World War I and relocated to the United States. In America, Helena found the perfect audience to embrace her innovative cosmetic and skincare lines with open arms and eager hearts.

She once said, *"All the American women had purple noses and gray lips, and their faces were chalk white from terrible powder. I recognized that the United States could be my life's work."*

Helena and Edward settled down with their sons in a luxurious apartment in Manhattan while maintaining a Tudor mansion in Greenwich, Connecticut. Within a year, Helena established four salons across America, and the harsh summer of 1915 inspired her to develop a line of creams to fight the effects of sun exposure. She reintroduced the Valaze cream with skin-cell regeneration formulas and countered her main competitor Elizabeth Arden's fitness rooms by introducing exercise programs in her salons.

Helena Rubinstein overshadowed most of her competitors during that period by emphasizing the scientific research and toxicity-testing her products underwent before reaching the market. She invested heavily in scientific research and development, and her staff was highly-trained. In 1917, Helena took a bold and dangerous risk by making all her products, cosmetics and skin care, available to the masses at affordable prices.

It was a risky move that denied exclusivity to her high-society patrons who enjoyed access to uniqueness. However it was always Helena's dream and core vision to impact the beauty rituals of the regular woman. This decision brought her innumerable struggles, which she overcame with relentless and unwavering determination. Helena decided to tour her salons and retailers nationwide, preaching her beauty philosophy and educating customers on using her products for effective results.

Edward continued glamourizing the brand's image with his publicity tactics, expanding Helena's network with Hollywood celebrities, New York high society, and Parisian artists from Greenwich Village. The couple would host the most exciting dinner parties, hosting celebrities, journalists, and artists like Francis Picabia, Henri Matisse, and Marcel Duchamp.

Since cinema significantly influenced American culture and lifestyle, Helena would recruit actresses from Hollywood's silent films to promote her products. Helena Rubinstein's collaboration with Theda Bara, America's most iconic sex symbol and vamp, is one of American history's most celebrated beauty collaborations. Inspired by Theda Bara's big, beautiful eyes, pronounced lips, and sultry performance in the 1915 film *A Fool There Was*, Helena introduced a bold makeup line titled *The Vamp*.

By 1920, Helena's cosmetic line was sold at all leading department stores, small-town beauty salons, local drug stores, pharmacies, and supermarkets worldwide, bearing the name Helena Rubinstein for the first time.

When the war ended, Helena returned to Europe to reopen her salon and introduce American innovations in salons and services across France, Germany, and other countries. In 1928, she realized that dividing her time between two continents was proving challenging, and she decided to sell her assets in the United States to Lehman Brothers for $7.3 million.

A year later, she bought back a controlling share in the American holdings after the stock market crash because she felt Lehman Brothers was damaging the quality-driven reputation of her brand.

Helena Rubinstein's Legacy

Helena Rubinstein witnessed the soaring heights of success, but the dazzling glamor didn't dissuade her from a hard day's work. She was dedicated to her work and deeply involved in running the business. Despite splurging millions on art, sculptures, and designer clothing, she remained true to her culture in more ways than one.

She would arrive at work on time every morning with a home-packed lunch in a neat brown bag. She was devoted to her dreams and focused on innovating the industry to leave a lasting imprint on the beauty sector. In Helena's own words, *"Work has indeed been my best beauty treatment. I believe in hard work. It keeps the wrinkles out of the mind and the spirit."*

Helena Rubinstein and Edward Titus divorced in 1938, and later that year, Helena married Russian Prince Artchil Gourielli-Tchkonia. Her marriage with Prince Artchil was a bond of creativity and love, and together, the couple took New York City by storm with an avant-garde product line under the House of Gourielli.

Helena lost her second husband in 1955, but despite being struck with grief, she remained consistent in observing her grueling work schedule and managing her philanthropic endeavors. In 1953, she founded the Helena Rubinstein Foundation, one of the world's largest medical research and health rehabilitation benefactors.

Helena's most profound legacy is more significant than her prized art collection, charitable organizations, and philanthropic involvement in the welfare of American Jewish and Israeli communities. Her legacy is her impact on the beauty industry, and her beauty philosophy that empowered women with the resources and tools to look and feel beautiful.

Helena Rubinstein's legacy is best described in her own words: *"I fell in love with beauty a long, long time ago, but what I wanted was to create beauty - not to be blinded by it."*

Chapter 2.2: Elizabeth Arden (1881 – 1966)

"It is remarkable what a woman can accomplish with just a little ambition."

— Elizabeth Arden

Elizabeth Arden is one of the most influential and prominent beauty innovators of the 20th century, accredited for endorsing the modern concept of using cosmetics and pampering oneself at beauty salons. Her rags-to-riches story inspires awe at the intricacies of her dream and her unyielding dedication to her passions. Amassing an empire worth over $60 million, Elizabeth Arden ranked among the wealthiest women of her time.

She helped American women realize the importance of nurturing themselves and taking care of their skin. She made it acceptable for women on the street to flaunt their beauty with bold makeup, dismantling the evangelical fears surrounding the idea of a woman using cosmetic products. She worked hard to raise awareness and change the restrictive perceptions of female beauty, encouraging American society to associate makeup with empowered and respectable women.

Elizabeth once said, *"I don't sell cosmetics; I sell hope"*, and her contributions to the beauty industry are a testament to this claim. She was the first to introduce some iconic innovations and beauty ideas that dominate the industry to this date, such as eye makeup for women, makeovers in stores, and travel-friendly products in smaller packaging.

Arden was a dedicated advocate of women's independence and a passionate participant in the suffrage movement. In fact, in 1912, Elizabeth played a key role by supplying over 15,000 marching suffragettes with dark red lipstick – a striking symbol of female emancipation when paired with the rally uniform.

Elizabeth believed that elegant makeup and a flawless complexion made modern women feel and look more confident. She encouraged all working women to groom themselves to appear more presentable. During World War One, she developed a specialized makeup kit for the American Marine Corps Women's Reserves, including her iconic red lipstick. The pigments used in the kit were designed to complement the hat stripe and tassels on the uniforms.

Humble Beginnings in the Village of Woodbridge

Elizabeth Arden was born Florence Nightingale Graham on December 31, 1878, in Woodbridge, Ontario, Canada. Named after her mother's her, the revered 19th-century nurse Florence Nightingale, she was one of five children in a poor, tenant-keeping household. Her father, William Graham, was the son of a modest Scottish farm-owner, while her mother, Suzan Tadd, belonged to an elite British family.

William Graham met Suzan Tadd on one of his racing trips to Cornwall, and it was love at first sight for the two lovers. Suzan came from a wealthy English family of landowners and ship manufacturers. Still, despite her parent's objections, she married a man far beneath her social standing, severing ties with her family.

William sold all his possessions to take his new wife to Canada, but in the 1870s, Toronto was not the finest city to welcome immigrants. William struggled to find a stable job, and with great difficulty, he managed to rent a small farm in the village of Woodbridge on the outskirts of northern Toronto. While William succeeded in providing his family with a small but consistent income, Suzan's health began to falter as her body struggled to adapt to the harsh weather, heavy labor, and poor living conditions.

As the couple welcomed five children into the family, Suzan's health declined, and she developed tuberculosis after giving birth to Florence. Overwhelmed by fatigue and sickness, Suzan had little choice but to delegate chores to the kids, asking them to perform menial jobs around the house and the farm.

Florence was responsible for caring for one of the horses – a job she wholeheartedly adored that inspired a lifelong love for horses and equestrian pursuits. When she turned six, Florence lost her mother, which was a devastating blow to a bright child who adored her mama and couldn't bear the loss of her departure.

It took time, but Florence, a lively and good-natured girl, overcame her loss and devoted herself to her education. She harbored big dreams of attending university and entering a respectable profession that would allow her to create a luxurious life for herself and her family. Her mother's sister had supported the family financially for a long time, but the support ran out before Florence reached high school.

This lack of financial support put the family in a quagmire, and Florence's dream of attending university was jeopardized. Grappling with uncertainty, Florence embraced the same career as her namesake and prepared herself to start training as a nurse. This endeavor demanded that she relocate to Toronto and enroll in nursing school.

Finding Her True Calling

Florence did not feel inspired at the nursing school; the career path depressed and scared her. However, Florence discovered her true calling for beauty and skincare at the school. She befriended a young man who worked for the hospital lab and was involved in developing a chemical formula to diminish the appearance of blemishes on the skin.

This acquaintance inspired the idea of developing a beauty cream, and within days, Florence had mapped out the entire production and distribution process. She would brew the formula herself and mail it to her customers. Armed with her dreams and equipped with innumerable ingredients, Florence quit nursing school and returned home to dedicate all her time to formulating her beauty elixir.

For a few months, her father tolerated the fishy experiments and horrible smell emanating from the kitchen, but eventually, he lost his patience and issued an ultimatum: Get a job or get married!

Disenchanted with the notion of matrimony, Florence took up odd jobs that could sustain her lifestyle with enough money to spare to continue formulating her beauty cream. She switched through multiple careers, working as a bank teller and later as a receptionist. She worked dedicatedly, but the nagging disappointment of failure shrouded her happiness.

Florence was struggling with the displeasure of her failures when her brother, who worked in New York City, invited her to look for opportunities there. She warmed to relocating to NYC – where millions had migrated to achieve the big American Dream. Her father forbade her from moving there, but in open defiance, Florence packed her bags and set out for New York City.

In 1908, a 30-year-old Florence arrived in New York City, feeling vivacious and looking much more youthful than typical for her age. Florence's physical beauty and charming personality worked in her favor when interviewing for potential jobs. It didn't take her long to land a job as a bookkeeper for a pharmaceutical company, E.R. Squibb and Sons.

Florence had applied for the job to advance her knowledge in chemistry and learn more about naturally-occurring chemicals and substances that heal the skin and enhance its outward appearance. Sadly, the chemists at E.R. Squibb and Sons weren't keen on discussing beauty creams and skincare formulas with the bookkeeper.

Disheartened and saddened, Florence switched careers and found a job as a cashier at a beauty salon. The salon belonged to Mrs. Eleanor Adair, one of the leading beauty experts of her time. Adair owned several elite beauty salons in New York City and supplied her beauty products worldwide. Eleanor Adair introduced Florence to the glamorous beauty business, inspiring her to learn about the crafts and techniques to beautify and nurture the skin.

Under Adair's guidance, Florence discovered a fascinating world of self-care and self-pampering. She learned about massage therapies and beauty culturists – a raging trend at the time. Beauty culturists were highly sought-after by high society women, for they claimed to revitalize the skin with special massages and scientific formulas.

Florence learned and learned until she was ready to move on and branch out on her own.

Salon with the Red Door

Instead of venturing out on her own, Florence fostered a partnership with a successful beauty entrepreneur, Mrs. Elizabeth Hubbard, who already had a lucrative line of skincare creams and tonics. Together, they opened a salon on NYC's Fifth Avenue and began catering to customers. The partnership didn't last long, and the two parted ways due to creative and financial conflicts.

Finally, Florence decided to take a giant leap of faith and make a solo venture. By now, she understood the importance of aesthetics and branding to captivate New York's high-society women. She believed that "Florence Nightingale Graham" was not a brand name that would attract women seeking exclusivity and glamor. She decided to pick a more appropriate name for the beauty business.

She took Elizabeth from her former partner's name, and "Arden" was inspired by one of her favorite Tennyson poems, *Enoch Arden.* Florence reinvented herself along with her name, and thus, the enigma of Elizabeth Arden was born.

In 1909, Elizabeth Arden took a $6,000 loan from her brother and opened her salon on Fifth Avenue, featuring the brand's trademark red door with a glistening brass plate. This was an iconic moment in the history of the beauty industry, for the opening of this salon marked the birth of the cosmetics industry in America. It was a pivotal moment for young girls and women across America, leading them toward the empowerment of self-representation and the freedom to beautify themselves as they desired.

During the early 19th century, it was not acceptable for "decent" and "nice" young girls to smear makeup on their faces or even apply creams to their skin. Elizabeth Arden addressed these societal perceptions with a crafty and clever approach, inspiring American society to alter its thinking by associating makeup with the image of a respectable lady.

Elizabeth Arden became one of the first beauty gurus to offer cosmetics and skin care products in department stores, alongside catering to walk-in customers in her salon. During this period, Elizabeth had many competitors, the most noteworthy of which was Helena Rubinstein. There was a heightened animosity and fierce competition between the two cosmetics maharishis, and Elizabeth would often refer to Rubinstein as "that woman".

Despite operating in a competitive industry where beauty salons and cosmetic products were abundant, Elizabeth maintained her influence and popularity. Unlike Rubinstein, who wanted to provide products for all women regardless of income and social status, Elizabeth focused on New York's elite and high-society socialites.

Elizabeth is credited with introducing the concept and term of the "beauty salon", transforming the beauty experience of a parlor into a more posh and upmarket venue for relaxation and self-pampering. This was a relatively new concept for women attracted by Elizabeth's salon concept, its relaxing ambiance, and an endless array of full-body rejuvenation treatments.

"Every woman has the right to be beautiful."

Elizabeth's most formidable challenges were changing societal notions and encouraging women to visit salons and invest in pampering themselves. In those days, it was downright scandalous for women, especially young girls, to paint their skin and emphasize their beauty attributes with bold and dark colors. Using any cosmetic or skincare product was deemed unladylike and equated with prostitutes and vamps.

Elizabeth worked tirelessly and campaigned feverishly to make cosmetics fashionable, ladylike, and respectable, expanding her market share and target audience by enormous proportions. She encouraged women to believe that glamor was not God-gifted, but a gift one acquires by looking after oneself.

She often said, "Every woman has the right to be beautiful", and actively inspired women to enhance their physical features and help nature with the right beauty elixirs and skincare formulas.

The Elizabeth Arden salon turned out to be a roaring success, and within six months of launching, Elizabeth could pay back the $6,000 she borrowed from her brother. In 1914, Elizabeth expanded her business by opening a salon in Washington, and later that year, she started selling her skincare products in various department stores across New York.

During this period, she launched two of her best-selling products that continue to serve as the cash cows of the Elizabeth Arden beauty empire: Ardena Skin Tonic and Cream Amoretta. In 1915, Elizabeth traveled to Paris to familiarize herself with French beauty culture and cosmetic lines. There, she discovered the European trends of eye shadow and mascara, becoming the first cosmetics producer to introduce eye shadow to American women.

The same year, Elizabeth tied the knot with Thomas Jenkins Lewis, a banker managing the company's wholesale division and expanding the business empire. The union lasted 19 years, but ended in a bitter divorce that prompted Lewis to work for Helena Rubinstein, Elizabeth's arch-nemesis.

Years later, Elizabeth remarried a Russian prince, and reports reveal that the marriage was performed during her lunch hour. Sadly, the marriage only lasted 13 months.

The year 1922 witnessed Elizabeth opening a salon in Paris, followed by a string of salons in European capitals and other countries. The Arden beauty empire was left untouched by the economic ravages of the Great Depression of the 1930s. Elizabeth's business was booming and generated impressive revenues of over $4 million annually. In fact, during the Depression, the flagship Elizabeth Arden salon was expanded to seven floors.

Where others saw economic difficulty, Elizabeth Arden saw an opportunity to expand and grow. In her words, "The depression is going to make a lot of manufacturers pull in, economize, cut down, and that leaves us a clear field."

Elizabeth responded to the economic turmoil by cutting prices and introducing many budget-friendly beauty treatments to help her struggling patrons maintain their lifestyles. When World War II broke out, The Elizabeth Arden beauty empire had an estimated net worth of $25 million.

Unrivaled Fame and Fortune

Elizabeth Arden's fame and fortune grew exponentially, and she operated luxurious salons and health spas worldwide. Her luxurious spas in Arizona and Maine charged customers the exorbitantly-high sum of $750 a week in exchange for high-end rejuvenation treatments and sought-after skincare rituals.

During this period, Elizabeth took enormous pride in her success. She lauded her own unwavering dedication by saying, "There are only three American names known in every corner of the globe: Singer sewing machines, Coca Cola and Elizabeth Arden."

During the 1940s, she began investing in horses, and at the peak of her success, she owned 150 horses. In May 1946, Elizabeth's beloved horse, Jet Pilot, won the Kentucky Derby, claiming a prize of over $600,000. It was around that time that Elizabeth was invited to grace the highly-coveted cover of Time Magazine in a lengthy piece about her success in cosmetics and her venture into the male-dominated realm of horse riding.

Time Magazine dubbed Arden "a queen who rules the sport of kings". During this period, Elizabeth's feud with her leading competitor, Helena Rubinstein, became a well-known industry phenomenon, and this battle for market supremacy lasted for five decades. Interestingly, Elizabeth Arden and Helena Rubinstein never met in person, despite competing against each other feverishly and socializing in the same circles.

This fierce competition compelled Arden and Rubinstein to prioritize creativity and innovating their product lines with new, cutting-edge cosmetics and skincare treatments.

After both her marriages divorced, Elizabeth devoted herself to her company and expanding her empire globally. She worked until the day before she died in 1966 and remained highly energetic, demanding, and vivacious until the end.

It is said that Elizabeth looked decades younger than her 87 years of age and remained actively involved in running her company till the very last day of her life. She was highly demanding of her employees and sought perfection in everything. She once said, "I only want people around me who can do the impossible."

Elizabeth would scrutinize every little detail and feature of her products. Once, she halted the production of an entire cosmetic line because the pink color of the packaging didn't feel right. This production halt cost the company a whopping $100,000!

Elizabeth Arden was devoted to delivering her customers the best quality, and for this purpose, she emphasized the need for strict adherence to quality controls. She was deeply invested in maintaining her brand's quality-driven image and sustaining customer loyalty toward her brand. She once said, "Repetition makes reputation, and reputation makes customers."

"Standards should be set by me and not imposed on me."

Elizabeth Arden's legacy stretches far beyond her brand, Elizabeth Arden Inc., which today is a wholly-owned subsidiary of Revlon Inc. Elizabeth was actively running her cosmetic empire when she passed away in 1966, leaving the brand with over 100 beauty salons worldwide and a line of over 300 cosmetic and skincare products.

Her loyal employees were bequeathed $4 million, and she left an estate worth $50 million, including a castle in Ireland and $1 million in jewels. Elizabeth Arden's legacy and reputation stem far beyond her beauty empire, deeply grounded in her dynamic role as an iconic innovator and liberator of women from evangelical shackles that denied their right to self-beautification and self-representation.

She was an ardent campaigner for women's rights and independence and a passionate innovator who transformed the beauty industry and women's relationship with cosmetic products. Elizabeth once said, "There is no reason for a woman to lose even one iota of her beauty."

She worked hard and tirelessly, pouring herself into running the empire, with 18-hour work days. Elizabeth loved learning more about cosmetics and recruited chemists to experiment with colorful pigments and develop specialized products.

Adren's beauty mantra revolved around women's power to beautify themselves, and she firmly believed that cosmetics and skincare products should combine nature and science to deliver an effective formula. Instead of covering up their concerns and blemishes, Elizabeth encouraged women to focus on enhancing and emphasizing their beauty assets.

Her concepts of beauty emphasized a focus on skincare, overall wellness, and physical fitness. Elizabeth often advised, "To achieve beauty, a woman must first achieve health."

Elizabeth Arden emulated this concept of beauty and health in the beauty spa she opened in Mount Vernon in 1934 – America's first destination spa and health club. Elizabeth actively practiced what she preached, and her youthfulness and undying energy were a testament to the fact that her formula for beauty and wellness worked wonders.

She followed a simple diet, with low-fat staples and nutrient-rich ingredients. Elizabeth exercised regularly to maintain her form and enhance the outward appearance of her skin with nutritious foods and nature-infused healing herbs. She encouraged and inspired women to prioritize their emotional and physical well-being to achieve beauty ideals and feel youthful.

Today, Arden is remembered as a dedicated and resilient fighter. She was a woman who transformed her life and achieved her dreams despite her humble beginnings as the daughter of a modest farm owner. Her lack of high school education and college degree did not stand in her way. She dismantled every obstacle fate tossed her way and continued flourishing even during the most challenging economic crises in the world.

Elizabeth Arden's most noteworthy biographer, Lindy Woodhead, described her larger-than-life personality as "a tough little Canadian who could swear like a longshoreman." Elizabeth always knew exactly what she wanted, and nothing could deter her from achieving utmost perfection in her craft.

Over the years, her brand succeeded in amassing affluent patronage worldwide, with innumerable celebrities and elite socialites dedicated to the Elizabeth Arden products. Some of the most devoted patrons of her brand include Marilyn Monroe, Marlene Dietrich, Queen Elizabeth II, Wallis Simpson, and Joan Crawford.

Chapter 2.3: Madam C. J. Walker (1867–1919)

"There is no royal flower-strewn path to success. And if there is, I have not found it, for whatever success I have attained has been the result of much hard work and many sleepless nights."

— Madam C. J. Walker

World-renowned as the first black woman millionaire in America, Madam C. J. Walker was a revered symbol of African American emancipation and female empowerment in the early 20th century. Madam made her fortune with a line of homemade concoctions to nurture and protect the luscious hair of Black women, giving birth to the highly acclaimed Walker System of preventing hair loss and growing voluminous manes.

Madam C. J. Walker's story is more than just a tale of a talented entrepreneur who capitalized on her skills of crafty marketing and self-promotion. Walker didn't just build a million-dollar business empire; the crux of her achievements lies in her philanthropic endeavors and contributions to the African American community.

Walker donated significant portions of her wealth to the Tuskegee Institute to fund scholarships for women and support multiple charities, including the Black YMCA and NAACP. Walker's contributions toward uplifting fellow Black women stand unrivaled. She was the first in the community to break free from destitution and embark on a successful entrepreneurial journey.

For Black women across America and worldwide, Madam C. J. Walker was the epitome of the big American dream, having built a business empire with her shrewd business acumen and savvy marketing skills. Walker founded Leila College, a business training institution named after her daughter, to teach women how to sell the brand's products and establish franchises.

Addressing young women of her time, Walker advocated:

The girls and women of our race must not be afraid to take hold of business endeavor and, by patient industry, close economy, determined effort and close application to business, wring success out of a number of business opportunities that lie at their very doors.

Walker empowered Black women by supporting entrepreneurial training and skill development, leading them toward financial freedom and self-identity. Having risen from the pits of poverty in the South, Madam C. J. Walker used her influence and wealth to advocate for uplifting African

Americans, women's empowerment, and ending heinous practices like lynching and slavery.

Born in Deep Destitution

On December 23, 1867, Minerva and Owen Breedlove, former slaves residing on a small farm just outside Delta, Louisiana, gave birth to a baby girl – their first free-born child and family member. The Breedlove family had four other children, Alexander, James, Louvenia, and Owen Jr., all born into slavery. But Sarah Breedlove was born free, with nothing but destitution and poverty to clip her wings and shackle her to impoverishment.

In 1863, four years before Sarah's birth, US President Abraham Lincoln abolished the barbaric system of slavery across America by signing the Emancipation Proclamation. Sarah was the first free member of her family, born as a free American citizen. Minerva and Owen believed Sarah was a Christmas gift, and her birth in the auspicious holiday season meant she would have a blessed and prosperous life. Little did they know Sarah was the most significant, unique gift for her family.

The family's joy at Sarah's birth was soon diminished by a crippling financial crisis that rendered them incapable of buying new clothes or fixing a rich Christmas feast for their kids. The Breedlove household survived on the pittance

Minerva and Owen made working in the cotton fields on the Madison Parish Farm, owned by Robert Burney.

Bollworms attacked the cotton crop the summer before Sarah's birth, eating out the plants just before harvest. Come Christmas, the Breedloves were struggling with food shortages, and Minerva had little time to care for herself and baby Sarah. The family of seven lived in a draft-riddled, one-room cottage with a leaky roof and a broken-down fireplace in the corner – their only source of heat and light.

The broken glass of the windows allowed the chill to seep into the cottage, leaving Baby Sarah and her siblings to shiver through the night. Despite their innumerable hardships, the Breedloves were devout Christians. The family would gather at the church each Sunday to hear Reverend Curtis Pollard's inspiring tales about the Promised Land and the path to heaven.

Having served as a senator for Louisiana state during the Reconstruction Period that granted black men the right to vote in the South, Reverend Pollard was a fierce advocate for African Americans' rights to educate themselves and achieve financial and political freedom.

The shackles of slavery had denied Minerva and Owen the right to learn how to read and write and build respectable careers for themselves, but they yearned to educate their daughters and sons because they firmly believed education was the key to freedom. However, educating little Sarah and her siblings wasn't possible, because Louisiana did not offer public education for African American people at the time.

White communities who did not want to compete with their former slaves for state resources like public education actively denied them opportunities for a better, more prosperous life. For instance, schools for black people were burned and razed to the ground, and in some areas, black teachers and their students were murdered in broad daylight.

Sarah's family was an African American plantation family, and this reality alone was the most significant barrier to educating her and her siblings. Like most other children who grew up on plantations, Sarah and her siblings worked in the cotton fields with their parents. Each child had a pivotal role in the seasonal duties, from planting the seeds in early spring to harvesting the cotton in late fall.

Sarah was put to work in the fields as soon as she was old enough to carry water and transport it to the laborers working in the field. By the time she reached six years of age, Sarah was put to work in the furrows, planting seeds as the older laborers pushed the plows. Louvenia and Sarah also helped their mother around the house, tackling multiple chores to assist an ailing Minerva.

Saturdays were designated as laundry days, and Minerva would take her two young daughters down to the riverbank with large wooden tubs and washboards. To supplement their income, the Breedloves washed the linens and clothes for the Burney family. For one dollar a week, Minerva, Louvenia, and Sarah would beat out the debris of the clothes of their white customers from dawn till dusk.

Beating the soil out of dirty linens was just as hard as picking cotton in the field. Washing the heavy cotton bed sheets and linen tablecloths demanded hard labor, for the clothes had to be soaked in scalding hot water, beaten with sticks to drive out the dirt, and washed with harsh lye soap. Minerva tried her best to make Saturdays a fun and light-hearted community event for her young daughters, singing along with the other women to keep them entertained.

Sarah loved listening to her mother croon, so awe-struck by her melodious voice that her mind wouldn't register the exhaustion of the laborious grind. The perfectly-synchronized rhythm of the singing women would blend with the whistles of the steamboats cruising the river, transporting little Sarah into her world.

Speaking of her early days years later, Walked said:

I am a woman who came from the cotton fields of the South. From there, I was promoted to the washtub. From there, I was promoted to the cook kitchen. And from there I promoted myself into the business of manufacturing hair goods and preparations.

Despite her family's great struggles, Sarah had a happy childhood, playing with her friend Celeste Hawkins and hunting crawfish in the bayous surrounding the plantation. Summers were all about fried fish, picnics, and Sunday mass at the Pollard Church, where Sarah sang in the choir, with her best friend Celeste holding onto her seat in the pews. In 1869, an overjoyed Sarah welcomed a baby brother named Soloman. However, this new family member strained the Breedloves' already-stifled financial circumstances.

Sarah and all her friends worked in the fields with their parents. The sharecroppers of the South had a hard, unfulfilling life that denied them access to basic necessities. Exhausting and never-ending labor, a poor diet, unsanitary living conditions, and no access to healthcare characterized their lives. The Breedlove family, like hundreds of other black plantation families, had little immunity to resist illnesses like cholera and yellow fever, which thrived on unhygienic food, unsanitary water, and mosquitos prevalent across the Mississippi riverbanks.

Thrust into Hardship and Hard Labor

In 1874, a 7-year-old Sarah lost her mother to the nationwide cholera epidemic, and within a few months, her father passed away as well.

Sarah and her siblings were devastated, and her older siblings tried their best to retain their position as laborers in the cotton fields. Still, without their parents, they weren't as valuable to the plantation owner. Alexander, Sarah's oldest brother, was the first to leave for Vicksburg in the hope of finding respectable work.

With her older brothers leaving the farm, little Sarah only had her sister Louvenia and younger brother Solomon to hold onto for love and support. After her parent's demise, she discovered the cruelty and harshness of the world around her, and she missed her doting mother and father terribly.

No one had a moment to spare for three frightened and deserted children struggling to survive alone on the plantation. Sarah would yearn to join the white children as they hopped along to school each morning, while she and Louvenia would spend every waking minute bending over the wash tubs and washing dirty linen to pay their rent and put food on the table.

Sarah was thrust into aggravated hardships and hard labor after her parent's demise, and life was more challenging than ever. In 1878, yellow fever struck again, claiming over 3,000 lives in what later came to be known as Vickburg's worst epidemic. The epidemic combined with financial ruin as the cotton crop was devastated, and Sarah, Louvenia and thousands of others lost their homes and means of livelihood.

The young girls had no choice but to relocate across the Mississippi River and move to Vicksburg to find decent work as housemaids or washerwomen, like countless other black Louisianan families. Back then, black families were deeply reliant on white plantation owners, who continued to enslave them. In the early 20th century, African Americans lived in fear of barbaric white terrorist groups like the Ku Klux Klan, with thousands struggling to escape the South and build new lives in North America.

The kind Reverend Pollard advised Sarah's brothers, Alexandar, James, and Owen, to relocate to St. Louis, a hustling and bustling city tucked at the northern tip of the Mississippi River, attracting scores of black families with the prospects of respectable employment and better living conditions. The three brothers moved to St. Louis in 1879 and, in a few years, saved enough to open a small barbershop.

With her brothers gone, Sarah felt abandoned and lonely. During this time, Louvenia, tired of feeling unsafe and subjecting her body to hard, back-breaking labor, married Jesse Powell.

Sarah began living on a farm with the newly-married couple, entering a tumultuous period. Powell was abusive and cruel and subjected the young girl to torture. Sarah had little choice but to run away and get married. At 14, Sarah found an escape from abuse in her marriage to Moses (Jeff) McWilliams. Explaining her choice to get married at such a young age, Sarah said she merely yearned for "a home of [her] own".

Moses, like Sarah, had not been able to attend school and did odd jobs here and there, like repairing train tracks in Vicksburg, plowing the cotton fields, and loading cotton bales onto boats at the harbor. Sarah was back to working in the cotton fields, picking cotton and supplementing her income by serving rich white women as a washerwoman.

On 6th June 1885, 17-year-old Sarah gave birth to a beautiful little girl named Leila. Leila was the light of her life, and even though she was working harder than ever, Sarah was the happiest she had ever been. The desire to give Leila a good, happy life consumed her thoughts, and the need to work hard became a passion rather than a necessity.

She knew if she worked hard enough, she could ensure Leila would have a different, easier, and happier life than her own. But fate had other plans for Sarah and Leila, for in 1887, Moses passed away shortly after Leila's second birthday. Some records maintain that Moses was a victim of the deadly race riots in Greenwich, Mississippi.

A New Chapter Brings New Opportunities

Widowed at 20, Sarah knew she couldn't return to her sister Louvenia's farm, where her cruel brother-in-law would torture the mother and daughter. She began warming up to move to St. Louis and join her brothers, who were thriving in the city with their barbershop. Despite living near the riverbanks and watching steamboats arrive and depart on the river, Sarah had never actually traveled farther than Vicksburg.

This was an exciting moment in her life, for St. Louis held the prospects of quality education for little Leila and well-paying jobs for Sarah. It was time for her to move on, and one fine morning, Sarah boarded a northbound riverboat with baby Leila held close to her chest. Sarah did not know the future but was optimistic it would bring her happiness and growth.

Arriving in St. Louis in 1888, Sarah and Leila initially squatted with her brothers until she managed to find work and rent an apartment. St. Louis was overflowing with migrants; an estimated 35,000 African Americans had relocated from the Deep South to find decent jobs. The city's black community supported over 100 businesses, including St. Louis' three newspapers.

In their first year in St. Louis, Sarah had to admit Leila at the St. Louis Colored Orphans Home several days a week while working as a housemaid – the primary career path for uneducated black women at the time. Being away from her child broke Sarah's heart, and she struggled hard to build a stable income as a washerwoman so she didn't have to entrust her daughter to someone else's care.

It took time, but Sarah McWilliams managed to build a stable life, where Leila went to school every morning and she worked hard to wash linens for affluent white families. Remembering her life from that period years later, Walker said:

As I bent over the washboard and looked at my arms buried in soapsuds, I said to myself, 'What are you going to do when you grow old, and your back gets stiff?' This set me to thinking, but with all my thinking, I couldn't see how a poor washerwoman was going to better my condition.

Sarah and Leila were dedicated members of the St. Paul African Methodist Episcopal (AME) Church, a powerful community center and the first church in St. Louis financed entirely by African Americans. In open defiance of the pre-Civil War laws that prohibited black people from learning to read and write, St. Paul's Church ran a secret, underground school for its members.

The church helped Sarah with financial assistance, food, and clothing and gifted her with a beautiful community of kind and generous women. One of these women, Jessie Robinson, was an elementary school teacher who doted on Sarah and recognized her desire to educate herself and become more than just an uneducated woman who washed scrubbed stains from dirty linens and ironed women's ruffled dresses using an open flame stove.

In 1894, Sarah married John Davis, an alcoholic with a raging temper. Overwhelmed by John's violent episodes of rage, Sarah's quest to help herself and improve her circumstances turned into a feverish passion. She started saving her income, and when Leila reached the 9th grade, Sarah managed to board a room at Knoxville College and afford a high school education for her daughter.

During this period, Sarah began actively participating in the church and its Mite Missionary Society, founded to assist needy members of the St. Paul church. Through the community, Sarah befriended well-educated African American women who were successful and actively involved in uplifting their communities. These encounters with prominent black leaders changed how Sarah dreamt of success and empowerment, giving her a new perspective to examine and improve her circumstances.

Sarah was an ardent admirer of Margaret Murray Washington, the President of the National Association of Colored Women (NACW). Her admiration for Madam Washington's immaculate outward appearance and enigmatic public speaking skills inspired confidence in Sarah, making her more self-conscious about her appearance. She recognized the links between a woman's physical appearance and inner strength, and while she could not afford expensive garb and finery, she wanted to improve her public image.

Sarah always dressed in neatly-ironed, squeaky-clean clothing to advertise her gifts as a skilled washerwoman. She took multiple measures to enhance her appearance, but her hair diminished her confidence. Sarah was deeply embarrassed by her hair, riddled with split ends and bald patches caused by an inflammatory scalp infection. Interestingly, such infections were prevalent among African American women at the time, given their lack of hair care, extremely stressful working conditions, and inadequate nutrition.

To make matters worse, most hair care products targeting black women at the time, such as Kinkilla, Queen Pomade, and La Creole Hair Restorer, featured harsh ingredients that did more harm than good. Sarah desperately needed the right product to heal her scalp and grow her hair with longer, thicker locks. But the more products she tried, the more convinced she was that the right hair product didn't exist – not for black women, at least!

During this time, Sarah began working as a sales agent for Annie Malone, an African American woman who developed and sold a popular hair product for black women, the Wonderful Hair Grower. Disappointed by the product's false claims and ineffectiveness, Sarah decided to take matters into her own hands. Working with Malone also made her realize her vocation for a similar venture, and she believed she had better sales tactics and marketing acumen than her employer.

Sarah experimented with many mixtures and pomades to straighten her curly locks and infuse them with nutrition and strength, but to no avail. Since Malone had an extensive network of sales agents throughout St. Louis, Sarah decided to leave Missouri and find a new market to increase her earnings while marketing Malone's products. She packed her bags and relocated to Denver, hosted by Lucy Breedlove, her widowed sister-in-law.

Woman on a Mission in the Mile High City

Hopeful that her sister-in-law Lucy and her four daughters would help her market and establish her new business across Colorado, Sarah got off the train at the Denver Union Depot one fine morning in July 1905. She was bewitched by Colorado's snow-sprinkled mountains and Denver's colorful and wide boulevards.

After living with Lucy's family for a few weeks, Sarah rented an attic room and became a Shorter Chapel African Methodist Episcopal Church member. She found a job as a cook for an affluent Denver resident, E.L. Scholtz. A Canadian-born American citizen, Schotlz owned Chicago's most significant and best-equipped pharmacy. The pharmacy offered various medications to fill doctors' prescriptions, alongside a well-stocked section of herbal tonics and homemade remedies. Sarah's employment at the Scholtz household was a turning point because the renowned druggist indulged her interest in herbal hair care remedies.

According to the family legend, Sarah routinely consulted Scholtz on various ingredients and herbs to refine and perfect her hair care products. She was eager to replace Annie Malone's products with her inventions and constantly experimented with formulas that were effective enough to sell.

One fine day, the formula with the "secret ingredient" came to her in a dream. Speaking to a reporter years later, Walker recalled the fateful moment of epiphany:

God answered my prayer, for one night I had a dream, and in that dream, a big black man appeared to me and told me what to mix up for my hair.

Some of the remedies were grown in Africa, but I sent for it, mixed it, put it on my scalp, and in a few weeks, my hair was coming in faster than it had ever fallen out. I tried it on my friends; it helped them. I made up my mind that I would begin to sell it.

Biographers and hair experts suspect this secret ingredient was probably sulfur – a compound known to stimulate hair growth and strength. Sarah combined her miracle-claiming product with a unique technique – heating a steel comb and running it through the curls with an ointment to straighten the hair.

After much experimentation, Sarah released three products she was incredibly proud of: the Glossine, the Vegetable Shampoo, and the Wonderful Hair Grower. As her creations began to sell, Sarah quit her job as a cook and began dividing her time between weekly laundry loads and product development. She actively sold her products with door-to-door campaigns, promoting her hair care line with a gifted skill that disarmed women and encouraged them to buy.

Sarah was a brilliant marketer, and one of her many incredible sales tricks included free treatments. She would offer to wash the customer's hair with her Vegetable Shampoo, followed by a thorough application of the Wonderful Hair Grower. Elated by the immediate results, customers would buy her products in large quantities. It didn't take long for Denver's black women to become loyal customers, resulting in high profits, which

Sarah plowed back into the business by running ads in the Colorado Statesman.

Sarah often used herself as a muse for her advertisements, using before and after pictures of her hair to show her product worked. By now, her business was thriving on door-to-door campaigns, direct mail orders, and personal sales trips to nearby cities and towns. As Sarah would unpin her well-groomed hair and cascades of soft, loose curls would tumble down to her waist, women would line up to listen to her advice and buy her products.

Despite moving to Colorado, Sarah had kept in touch with an old friend from St. Louis, including Charles Joseph Walker, a newspaper sales agent. Sarah corresponded with Charles regularly and kept him updated on the progress of her business. C.J., as he was known among friends, would provide a reliable supply of practical advice, and in 1905, he arrived in Denver to meet her.

On 4th January 1906, Sarah and C. J. Walker tied the knot in a humble ceremony hosted at a friend's home, and Sarah officially became Madam C. J. Walker. Charles' sales acumen and experience as a newspaper sales agent benefitted Sarah's budding business enormously. He encouraged her to rename her star product, thus creating the infamous Madam Walker's Wonderful Hair Grower.

A Booming Family Enterprise

It is pertinent to understand that women, especially black women, had no rights in the early 20th century. America during this period was riddled with gender and racial discrimination, and black women fell at the far end of the political and social spectrum, denied the right to own property or run a business unless permitted to do so by their fathers or husbands.

When her hair care business began bringing in an income of $10 a week, Charles Walker was convinced that Sarah's entrepreneurial dream had matured and her products had reached their full potential. But Sarah was adamant about achieving more. She was confident that if she could only travel and market the product across other cities and states, she could expand her consumer base considerably.

Her husband and friends tried to convince her against this madness, as they called it, but Sarah was undeterred. One fine September in 1906, a determined Sarah C. J. Walker and a reluctant Mr. Walker visited nine states. They marketed her products to women in Louisiana, Mississippi, New York, and Oklahoma.

Within a few months, their weekly sales soared to $35, and their consumer base increased considerably. The 21-year-old

Leila, who had just graduated from Knoxville College, relocated to Denver to manage her mother's direct mail orders while the couple traveled nationwide. Leila's inclusion in the business lent an aura of sophistication to the marketing tactics and sales pitches. The company became a family enterprise with Leila, Lucy, and her four daughters, Anjetta, Gladis, Mattie, and Thirsapen, working hard to handle the influx of orders pouring in from all corners of the country.

Being on the road and interacting with new customers inspired Madam Walker to recruit and train women as sales agents to expand her business. The spring of 1908 witnessed Madam Walker's business soaring to new heights, with hundreds of sales agents bringing her company $400 a month. The direct mail orders had grown exponentially, prompting Walker to relocate her company to Pennsylvania City to gain access to a larger community of African American women.

Walker established her office on Pittsburgh's Wylie Avenue, a hub for the city's thriving African American community and countless businesses owned by affluent black families. Sarah's days of working as a laundress were far behind her. In Pittsburg, she was the elegantly-dressed and business-savvy Madam C. J. Walker – a respectable businesswoman bursting with ideas and schemes to expand her booming business.

In 1908, Leila, Sarah, and Charles combined creative forces to launch a beauty parlor and a training institute for the Walker sales agents, and thus, the Lelia College of Beauty Culture was born. The graduates of this institute were certified as "hair culturists", cementing the brand's reputation for selling products that "cultivated" and nurtured the hair.

Within two years of opening, Leila College graduated hundreds of hair culturists, supporting the ambitions and dreams of young black women who did not wish to work as housemaids, cleaners, and laundresses.

Becoming America's First Black Woman Millionaire

In 1910, the Pennsylvania Negro Business Directory published a cover story on Madam C. J. Walker, dubbing her one of the "most successful businesswomen of the race in this community".

The photographs accompanying the feature depicted an urbane and poised Sarah, clad in a high-necked, floor-trailing dress with long tresses coiffured to the inch and pinned elegantly atop her head. Sarah's designer attire and confidence resembled the white women whose clothes she had spent years washing along the riverbanks.

She had achieved her dream of financial freedom and prosperity and ranked among Pittsburgh's most affluent and influential black residents. Walker actively gave back to her community, advocating for black women's right to education, respectful careers, and financial freedom. The same year, she relocated to Indianapolis, Indiana after eyeing the state's market as the perfect playground to capitalize on America's largest inland manufacturing hub.

In Indianapolis, Walker established a factory, another campus of the Lelia beauty school, and a hair and manicure salon. Within a year, Madam Walker became one of Indianapolis's prominent citizens, grabbing nationwide headlines for her philanthropic contributions, including her $1000 donation for the construction of the colored YMCA.

In 1916, Walker relocated to New York to conquer NYC and its surrounding towns after entrusting the operations of her factories and salons in Indianapolis to two loyal employees. As the business continued to boom and grow exponentially, Walker introduced a system of organizing all her employees into city and state clubs. In 1917, she established the Walker Hair Culturist Union of America.

Having chosen New York as her last residence, Madam Walker felt the need to commemorate her success with a mansion that would serve as an example of what a black woman could accomplish in the early 20th century. She bought a four-and-a-half-acre estate at Irvington on the banks of the Hudson River and hired an African American architect, Vertner W. Tandy, to work on her luxurious villa.

The mansion in Long Island was stunning, and its construction cost a whopping $350,000. Named Villa Lewaro, the estate featured spacious bedrooms, a luxe swimming pool, and beautifully-manicured Italian gardens. Walker lovingly decorated the home with furnishings and fixtures from around the world, including a rare Weber piano with a gold leaf and a complimentary Victrola.

Madam C. J. Walker's philanthropic ambitions grew more meaningful as her fortunes rose, with hefty donations to numerous charities supporting African American communities nationwide. She was one of the leading donors to the Indianapolis Alpha Home and Flanner House and a prominent beneficiary of the Bethel AME Church.

Walker was the 20th century's leading advocate and champion of education for African American, especially young girls who sought better life prospects. She donated generously to Mary McLeod Bethune's Daytona Educational and Industrial School for Negro Girls in Florida, the Tuskegee Institute, the Palmer Memorial Institute in North Carolina, and the National Association for the Advancement of Colored People.

Madam C. J. Walker is remembered as an advocate for African Americans' right to education and for her protest against racial discrimination. In 1915, she filed a lawsuit to register a legal protest against rampant racial discrimination at a local theater in Indianapolis.

Later in 1917, Madam Walker made national news by representing African Americans at the Benevolent Association, urging the members to denounce lynchings prevalent in the South. Walker is also known to have donated $5000 to support the anti-lynching movement led by The National Association for the Advancement of Colored People (NAACP).

Madam C. J. Walker's life achievements and philosophy is best explained in her own words. Addressing the public at a gathering, she said:

I am not merely satisfied in making money for myself, for I am endeavoring to employ hundreds of women of my race. ... I want to say to every Negro woman present, don't sit down and wait for the opportunities to come. Get up and make them!

Chapter 2.4: Annie Malone (1869-1957)

"Chicago, in my opinion, is the capital of Negro America. The people here are accomplishing things. The atmosphere is one of commercial striving, endeavor and promise."

— Annie Minerva Turbo Malone

Historians often dispute Madam C. J. Walker's status as America's first black woman millionaire, arguing that this honor rightfully belongs to Annie Minerva Turbone Malone, a prominent African American entrepreneur, educator, inventor, and philanthropist. Two years younger than Madam Walker, Annie Malone was Walker's former employer and one of America's most successful black businesswomen.

Annie developed a unique line of hair care products, transforming her love for hair pampering and styling into a million-dollar business empire, including the world-famous Poro College, where she taught students her patented self-care Poro method.

Annie Turnbo Malone is remembered as a trailblazer who made far-reaching and impactful contributions to uplifting

African American communities through her commercial and educational enterprises.

Throughout history, Western hair care, skin care, and cosmetic manufacturers have always neglected the needs of women of color, compelling them to concoct their own remedies and solutions. Annie Malone was one of the first African American women to introduce specialized products tailored to the needs of black women.

She was the first to draw attention to the damaging effects of mainstream hair care products, helping her African American clients overcome hair loss and scalp damage. Annie was a gifted and self-taught chemist and herbalist, and her talents allowed her to earn millions through a successful line of hair care products.

But Annie Malone wasn't interested in minting money alone; instead, she wanted to use her wealth to uplift her fellow African Americans, using her wealth to fund multiple charities and nonprofits. While Malone isn't a household name like Madam C. J. Walker, her contributions and legacy have inspired generations of young African American entrepreneurs, including Madam Walker, to prioritize and pursue their dreams.

In 1920, Annie Malone owned a business worth $14 million, with her products sold door-to-door with an extensive network of skilled Poro agents spanning multiple cities and towns. She is credited with inventing the revolutionary hair oils and straighteners that allowed black women to straighten their curls without damaging their hair and scalp.

Many have dubbed Annie Malone the Oprah Winfrey of her time. This lesser-known African American businesswoman overcame many treacherous adversities and challenges from the rampant gender and racial discrimination in 19th and 20th century America.

Young Hair Care Aficionado

Annie Minerva Turnbo Malone was born on August 9, 1869 to parents Isabella and Robert Turnbo in Metropolis, Illinois. Formerly enslaved people, Isabella and Robert, were eager to transform their lives and provide their children with education and decent livelihoods. The beginning of the Civil War provided them with the opportunity they sought.

Robert signed up for the First Kentucky unit of the Union Army while Isabella, along with her ten children, escaped Kentucky – a neutral territory that maintained slavery. With the shackles of slavery far behind them, Isabel secretly traveled along the Ohio River until she found refuge in Metropolis, Illinois. Robert joined his family shortly after, and the couple established a small farm.

Annie came into the family when her parents and siblings had bid adieu to their days in slavery and found a place they could call home. Unfortunately, the days of happiness and joy didn't last long, for both Isabella and Robert succumbed to illness and passed away, one after the other. A young, orphaned Annie came under the care of her older sister, Ada Moody.

Annie relocated to Peoria with Ada and began studying at the local school. She loved learning and had a keen interest in chemistry. However, Annie missed a great deal of school because of a recurring illness that kept her bedridden and sickly throughout her school years. While she couldn't finish high school and get a degree, Annie found craftier ways to satisfy her thirst for knowledge.

Chemistry fascinated Annie considerably, and she spent hours bending over utensils filled with various compounds and herbs, experimenting with concoctions and poultices. Mother Moody, Annie's aunt and an escaped enslaved person like her parents, piqued the little girl's interest and supplied her with the knowledge she craved. Mother Moody was a seasoned herbalist who would take Annie on exciting herb-picking adventures in the woods.

Mother Moody and Annie would spend hours in the forest, gathering a wide assortment of herbs and plants known to have beneficial properties. Back home, Mother Moody would separate each herb in her kitchen and regale a fascinated Annie with the remarkable properties of each plant. This first-hand knowledge helped Annie understand which herbs and plants most benefit the hair.

Annie had a fondness for hair care and styling as a young child. She would spend hours beautifying and nurturing her and her sisters' hair, adorning them with elegant hairstyles and pleats. She was highly aware of the differences in hair color tones and textures and sought new ways to pamper and style them.

As her knowledge of herbal concoctions grew, Annie began experimenting with products to help black women address their unique hair care needs. She was obsessed with the idea of finding a hair-straightening solution that didn't cause any damage to the scalp and hair follicles.

During that period, black women were discarding their natural hair textures and typical styling techniques like braids and plaits because these hairdos became synonymous with their days in slavery. The traditional braided cornrow hairdos symbolized black women working in the fields. The abolishment of slavery meant equality and better prospects for African Americans, and women wanted to commemorate their newfound freedom with straight hair.

The straight-hair look was in high demand when Annie was a young teenager, with black women eager to embrace more progressive and stylish hairdos that would symbolize their freedom and independence. Back then, the beauty and hair care industry was oblivious to black women's unique hair and skin care needs. Most products targeting African American consumers were manufactured with low-quality ingredients, which did more harm than good.

Women typically straightened their hair with age-old home remedies like lye soap, heavy oils, bacon grease, goose fat, butter, and even the carding combs used on sheep. These methods were hazardous for the scalp, resulting in unprecedented damage to hair follicles and the skin underneath.

Annie sought to change these drastically-harmful practices and equip the women with the right products and tools to take pride in their beautiful manes. The first product she developed was a liquid shampoo, which didn't satisfy Annie's quest for a toxin-free hair straightening product to strengthen hair follicles and nourish the scalp from deep within.

"The Great Wonderful Hair Grower"

Annie and her sisters, Ada and Laura, left Peoria for the vibrant town of Lovejoy, Illinois, America's oldest predominantly-African American community, famous as the place where Elijah Lovejoy, a renowned abolitionist, was slain by a horde of pro-slavery activists in 1837. Lovejoy, modern-day Brooklyn, provided Annie with the perfect learning environment and a thriving community of black women desperate for hair care products to beautify their unruly manes.

Annie began educating herself on the different hair textures and tones of diverse people of color. She set up a makeshift laboratory to experiment with various chemicals and herbs and equip herself with practical skills to address common hair concerns. Annie was set on developing the perfect hair-straightening solution that didn't contain goose fat, greasy oils, or butter!

She developed a multitude of lotions, ointments, hair salves, and potions to heal the scalp from deep within and combat hair falls with healthier locks. Finally, she developed the ace formula that would turn her from a hair care aficionado to the owner of a million-dollar company: The Great Wonderful Hair Grower.

By this time, Annie began styling herself as a beauty care specialist and distributing her products among family and community members for testing and evaluation. At the age of 20, she developed an extensive line of beauty and hair care products that were specifically tailored to the needs of African American women. The line included hair oils, liquid shampoos, hair stimulants, relaxers, straightening products, and her best-selling hair growth-boosting formula, the Great Wonderful Hair Grower.

The concept of a female entrepreneur, let alone a black female business owner, was an anomaly during the early 20th century, even though multiple powerful women were actively penetrating the entrepreneurial arena and thriving on consumer-driven success. But these women lacked the resources to support and uplift their entrepreneurial endeavors.

Like innumerable other female entrepreneurs of her time, Annie lacked access to conventional marketing and product distribution channels. But much like the other female trailblazers of her time, Annie had a dream, and nothing could deter her from chasing its actualization. She began a door-to-door campaign to introduce her products throughout the community, and it didn't take long for her highly-effective hair care line to attract scores of loyal customers.

Her creations spread across Lovejoy like wildfire in a jungle, resulting in unparalleled popularity that brought women to her doorstep. She emerged as the community's go-to expert for hair care advice, and her products became famous for healing scalp sores and acute hair loss.

Despite her sister Ada's disapproval and disdain, Annie continued expanding her customer base and eventually managed to stock her products at local stores and pharmacies. She opened her first storefront in Madison and expanded her product lineup with a series of beauty products. During this period, Annie Malone developed the pressing comb, an invention still popularly used worldwide and patented under her name.

Phenomenal Success in St. Louis

In 1902, Annie Malone relocated to St. Louis, Missouri, home to America's fourth-largest African American population at the time. In St. Louis, Annie sought to expand her business and customer base, and she had chosen the perfect market.

St. Louis was a hustling and bustling hub of commercial and industrial activity. Annie established her hair care salon in Ville, an upmarket neighborhood near downtown St. Louis. She hired three black women as her assistants, delegating her door-to-door marketing duties to them. Annie improved her sales technique to appeal to the relatively more progressive and financially independent consumer audience in St. Louis.

Her assistants would arrive at the customer's doorstep with four Turnbo products, winning them over with free giveaways and samples. Annie trained the assistants to provide a variety of hair treatments and comprehensive, step-by-step product demonstrations to help customers use the products effectively. Annie had to resort to unconventional marketing and promotional techniques, because being a black woman in the

20th century denied her access to conventional marketing and sales channels.

Rather than displaying her products at local stores, she could only capitalize on door-to-door campaigns, forced to meet her customers at their doorsteps instead of the marketplace. These barriers and challenges did not deter Annie Turnbo – instead, they fueled her determination to find crafty new tricks to expand her reach. She would address large crowds of black women from a buggy, hold press conferences, and print newspaper advertisements for African Americans.

In 1903, Annie Turnbo tied the knot with Nelson Pope, and later that year, she opened her first store in St. Louis on 2223 Market Street. Annie divorced her husband in 1907, and her business achieved exponential growth and success, serving black women throughout the Midwest and tapping new markets nationwide and as far away as the Caribbean.

After opening her first store in St. Louis, Annie decided to tour the Southern states to promote her products and connect with African American communities. This sales tour proved highly lucrative, and Annie continued to recruit black women everywhere she went, training them to sell her products. She developed an extensive system of direct mail orders, mailing her products to African American women throughout the South.

The 1904 World's Fair was a dynamic turning point in Malone's business expansion. It transformed St. Louis into a bustling global marketplace with consumers, retailers, and wholesalers from all over the country and far-flung corners of the world. Annie set up a retail outlet with her most skilled assistants interacting with the visitors, offering demonstrations and free-of-charge treatments to acquire new customers.

Visitors loved Annie's products, and aside from amassing an extensive list of new customers to add to her mail subscription list, Malone was bursting with innovative marketing ideas. Her sales experience at the World's Fair made her realize that her product had the potential to generate far more revenue if only she could establish nationwide distribution and marketing channels.

Annie expanded her outreach programs from door-to-door campaigns to community centers and African American churches, enticing potential customers with free hair care sessions and scalp treatments. She doubled her spending on advertisements in nationwide black newspapers and planned sales trips to cities and towns across the South and the Midwest.

It is pertinent to note that Annie Turnbo Malone toured the South at a tumultuous time when the Southern states were gripped with racial discrimination and violence. Undeterred and unfazed by the burgeoning waves of racially-charged violence, a high-spirited Annie would remain on the road for weeks, holding press conferences in women's clubs and giving product demonstrations in African American churches.

Everywhere Annie went, she left a trail of highly-trained and financially-independent black women working as local sales agents marketing the Turnbo products and profiting on the commissions. By 1910, Annie established a nationwide distribution and marketing network, turning her small-scale hair care venture into a million-dollar enterprise.

But it wasn't just about money for Annie Turnbo Malone. This robust black entrepreneur was deeply invested in the upward mobility of her community. She recruited and trained black women to boost her sales network. Still, her underlying motive was empowering the women of her community, steering them toward self-care, financial independence, and upliftment.

Annie firmly believed that if African American women groomed themselves and cared for their physical appearance, they could attract better life prospects. She thought that the physical beauty of black women would bolster their self-confidence, self-esteem, and self-respect, increasing their opportunities to succeed.

She wanted the women of her community to seek gratifying career choices that didn't involve washing clothes or laboring in fields. Annie actively preached and motivated black women to chase their dreams and achieve economic independence.

Poro is Born

Annie introduced the Poro Method of hair styling, and instead of urging women to lather their hair with greasy oils and poultices, she had a clear and straightforward motto: "Clean Scalps Mean Clean Bodies".

Unlike other hair care specialists of her time, Annie emphasized the significance of hygiene, encouraging her customers to ensure their scalps were clean and their hair follicles unclogged at all times. It didn't take long for the Poro Method of hair care to spread through the South like wildfire, introducing black women to a simple strategy to style their hair and feel confident. Annie encouraged a healthy diet, good hygiene, scalp massages, and correct use of her products for best results.

Annie Malone introduced this technique as "Poro", inspired by the West African devotional organization prevalent across Liberia and Sierra Leone. The Poro society is dedicated to self-disciplining and achieving spiritual ascension through the physical and mental enhancement of the body. The society's physical cleansing and beautification rituals inspired Annie's ideology behind adopting the term "Poro".

She wanted to connect her brand's identity and ideology with the physical and spiritual devotion to self-enhancement preached by Western Africa's Poro society. Even though connecting with African roots wasn't precisely *a la mode* in early 20th-century America, Annie Malone wanted her business to empower and inspire her African American community by facilitating a deep-rooted emotional and spiritual connection.

Her agents were dubbed the Poro Agents. Annie encouraged them to connect with their multigenerational African roots to carve out a niche and distinguish the Poro brand from other hair care lines. For Annie Malone, Poro was more than just a beauty and hair care brand. It was an economic and ideological medium to facilitate the upward mobility of black women, freeing them from the shackles of low-paying and demeaning jobs as domestic workers.

Back then, Poro agents earned ten times more than washerwomen and housemaids, living independent lives on their own terms and distinguished by their elegant attire and neatly-coiffed hair. Annie advised her agents to take special care of their physical appearance to reflect the brand's ethos, encouraging them to strengthen their self-esteem and self-confidence to achieve their desired success.

Around this time, Annie recruited Sarah McWilliams, her most famous client and recruit, who later became the legendary Madam C. J. Walker. Walker had struggled with baldness, hair loss, and dandruff for years, and Annie was the one to diagnose her with psoriasis.

After examining her hair and scalp, Annie realized that she had been using harsh alcohol-based shampoos and tonics, which worsened her condition. She introduced Walker to her products and advised her to wash her hair regularly, gently massaging her scalp and cleaning the hair follicles with a sulfur-based treatment. She also urged Walker to adopt a healthy diet with clean eating patterns and use her oils to massage the scalp and strengthen the hair follicles.

Walker embraced the Poro method, and her short hair grew past her shoulders for the first time without becoming brittle or dry. Happy with the results and the prospects of a stable income, Walker became a Poro agent, but it didn't take long for her ambitions to grow and exceed those of her employer and mentor.

Madam C. J. Walker liked Annie's business model and products but didn't believe in her marketing strategy. An ace marketer and crafty sales agent, Walker believed she could do better and quadruple the profits with a similar business model. It is widely thought that Walker stole one of Annie Malone's products, the Wonderful Hair Grower, and began selling it in Denver without changing the name. Eventually, the two had a falling out and went their separate ways.

Interestingly, Walker wasn't the only one counterfeiting Annie Turnbo's products, and Annie copyrighted her beauty and hair care lines under the brand label Poro to prevent counterfeit sales.

In 1914, Annie Turnbo-Pope married Aaron Eugene Malone and appointed her husband as Chief Manager and President of her company. Four years later, in 1918, Annie created her magnum opus, the Poro College of Beauty.

The Poro College was an African American landmark and the first institution that educated and trained African American beauticians and hair care specialists. The complex was a world of its own, featuring a cosmetology school, a vibrant community center, a dormitory, a chapel, an office space, a retail outlet, and a manufacturing facility.

The students and staff would reside in the dormitory, and the complex offered multiple recreational amenities, including a gymnasium, a bakery, and ambient lounging space. Poro College even featured a 500-seat auditorium and a rooftop garden. In 1920, Annie expanded the complex to add an ice cream parlor, a tailor shop, a barber shop, a confectionary shop, and a millinery store.

Poro College didn't just expand in terms of amenities and commercial activities. It also employed over 200 staff members to run the operations. At the height of Annie Malone's success, Poro College served as the beating heart of the St. Louis African American community, enveloping black families with commercial, cultural, and social activities.

Poro College didn't take long to expand to multiple cities and states, expanding the Poro Agents network to over 75,000 female beauticians, hair care experts, and sales agents.

During this period, Annie was making millions from nationwide and regional sales, and during the 1920s, her estimated net worth was around $14 million. According to The Philadelphia Tribune, Annie Turnbo Malone was the biggest African American taxpayer in the nation, having paid about $40,000 in taxes during the mid-1920s.

A Failing Marriage and Declining Empire

Annie Malone was a generous benefactor and patron of her community. She donated millions to various African American causes, supporting education, career progression, and economic independence for her community. Her generosity garnered her immense respect in her community, but it also proved to be a catalyst for the financial ruin of her business.

Journalists believe two main catalysts fueled the decline of Annie Malone's multi-million business empire. Firstly, her civic engagements and philanthropic endeavors distributed her wealth to multiple organizations, compelling her to donate a significant chunk of her earnings. Secondly, Annie tied herself up in charitable endeavors and community-focused engagement, leaving her husband and dishonest managers to run the day-to-day affairs of her business.

In 1921, Annie and Aaron Malone became entangled in a bitter divorce, which evolved into a six-year-long emotionally draining power struggle over the financial control of the Poro business empire. In 1927, Aaron Malone officially filed for divorce, demanding a 50% share of the business. Aaron claimed he was primarily responsible for Annie's success considering the affluent contacts he brought to strengthen the business.

Aaron Malone had an affluent social network of power-makers and leaders, courting prominent African American leaders and lunching with politicians, none of whom hesitated to support him in his bitter and highly-publicized divorce from Annie Turnbo Malone.

This was a devastating period for Annie, who was losing both her family and the prospects of losing half her business – an empire she had worked day and night to build from the humblest of beginnings.

Annie's devotion to her community, empowerment of black women, and charitable organizations had blessed her with a fiercely-supportive tribe. Throughout the divorce, Annie was surrounded by her loyal Poro agents, church leaders, and African American philanthropists. Even Mary McLeod Bethune, the President of the National Association of Colored Women, stepped up to support Annie Malone. The press and journalists also helped Annie counter the negative publicity stemming from this harrowing debacle.

The support of powerful women helped Annie overcome this situation and keep her business with a negotiated settlement of $200,000. Three years after paying off Aaron Malone, Annie bid goodbye to her life in St. Louis and relocated her business empire to Chicago.

In Chicago, Annie bought four mansions erected in a row, turning the entire block on Chicago's South Parkway into the Poro Block. Her palatial-style mansion at 4411 South Parkway (modern-day King Drive) once served as the residence of John R. Thompson, an affluent businessman who forbade black men and women from eating at his restaurants. Annie Malone's ownership of this property was an ironic twist of fate, much like the burgeoning African American influence on America's economic, literary, political, and social foundations.

Annie was welcomed to Chicago with a warm reception and a lavish ball attended by the crème de le crème of Illinois society, including Robert S. Abbott, the founder of Defender. Annie established a campus of the Poro College in Chicago and busied herself with running the company's day-to-day affairs.

Unfortunately, Annie's success in Chicago paled considerably compared to the company's growth and revenues when it was headquartered in St. Louis. Even though Annie continued to travel across the country to find new markets for her product, she struggled to manage the financial obligations of ensuring profitability.

As she traveled extensively, Annie left her company's financial affairs in the hands of unscrupulous employees and dishonest managers who exploited her trusting nature. During the 1930s, Annie became embroiled in a series of damaging lawsuits, one of which was filed by an employee attempting to take credit for Poro's success. Settling these lawsuits claimed much of Annie's health and wealth, forcing her to sell much of her property in St. Louis.

Annie was devastated by her second divorce, and the potential loss of her business was too much for her to bear. But this wasn't the end of her struggles – it was only the beginning.

Malone incurred a hefty fine from the government due to some unpaid excise duties and real estate taxes, which crippled her financial health and forced her to sell off assets. And in January 1940, Annie's Chicago mansion was destroyed by a raging fire, resulting in over $50,000 worth of damages.

By 1943, Annie owed an enormous debt of approximately $100,000, and the Internal Revenue Service (IRS) served her a lien. She fought a hard and tumultuous 8-year-long battle to retain her company but lost Poro to her creditors and the US government.

In 1951, the government and other creditors took control of Poro, selling off most of the company's assets and holdings to pay off the debt. The campuses of Poro College in St. Louis and Chicago were demolished, and the Poro Block was also sold off. Poro Clubs and Poro Beauty Agents continued working and selling the products while colleges across the country were shut down, one after the other. The last Poro college to shut down was the campus in Cincinnati, demolished in 1989.

On 10th May 1957, Annie Minerva Turnbo Malone died from a stroke at the Provident Hospital. At her death, over 30 Poro

Beauty Colleges were still operational. Today, Annie's legacy is often overshadowed by the success of her more famous and sensational client and employee, Madam C. J. Walker. Still, Annie Malone certainly hasn't been forgotten by any means!

Annie Malone's Inspiring Legacy

Annie Malone was one of the most prominent African American philanthropists in the early 20th century, maintaining franchised outlets of her company in North and South America and stretching her empire as far as Africa and the Philippines.

Despite her staggering wealth, she lived humbly and did not squander her wealth on frivolous luxuries. Annie donated a significant portion of her fortune to uplift African Americans, funding many initiatives focused on education and empowerment. Annie Malone donated $25,000 to facilitate the construction of St. Louis Colored YWCA and emerged as the most significant African American donor of Howard University after contributing $25,000 to the institution's funds.

Annie Malone was generous and kind, showering her family, friends, and employees with attention, care, and love. She educated her nieces, nephews, and even her employees' children and bought homes for her siblings and friends. The Poro Beauty Agents worked hard because Annie rewarded their dedication with expensive gifts, showering them with commissions for their punctuality and sales targets.

From 1919 to 1943, Annie served as the board president of the St. Louis Colored Orphans Home, shouldering the construction and operational costs of the orphanage. In 1919, she donated $10,000 to construct a new building; later, in 1922, she invested in a facility in the historic Ville quarters to expand the orphanage. In 1946, the facility was officially renamed the Annie Malone Children and Family Service Center, dedicated to her legacy and memory.

Today, St. Louis keeps Malone's legacy and memory alive by hosting the Annual Annie Malone May Day Parade on 20th May – a fun-filled gala and fundraiser. This event marks America's oldest black parade. The Annie Malone Children and Family Center is still functional and has helped uplift innumerable black children and families cornered by societal prejudices and economic challenges.

Annie Malone's story is best summed up by the comments of Theresa Shields, administrative coordinator of the Annie Malone Foundation and organization of the St. Louis parade. Shields is quoted to have said:

Annie Malone was the first Black millionaire. A lot of people don't know about her because of Madam C.J. Walker. She took a lot of Malone's products and took credit for them. It's sad.

In 2002, the DuSable Museum of African American History celebrated Annie's life and legacy with a 6-month-long exhibition, the Annie Malone: Black Beauty Culture Pioneer and Millionaire.

Chapter 2.5: Anna Sutherland Bissell (1846-1934)

"Trusting her own judgment even in the face of discouragement, she had great self-reliance, believed in enterprise, and had faith in her own resources; and so ends on this high note a beautiful life such as is given to few women to enjoy; or to pass on to her descendants a legacy so rich in example, in memories so happy, or in inspiration so great."

— Anna Bissell McKay (daughter of Anna Sutherland Bissell)

Remembered as the first female CEO in the history of America, Anna Sutherland was a pioneer in advertising and branding, inspiring advertisers with her clever branding and sales techniques to this day.

Her crafty branding strategy transformed her husband's carpet sweeper manufacturing business, expanding a national brand to international markets with consumers worldwide after she took over the company's reins following her husband's death.

Anna Sutherland Bissell was a savvy and seasoned business leader, well-versed in money-minting, from advertising and branding to manufacturing, sales, and distribution. She was a masterful sales agent and brand promoter, managing the marketing side of the business while her husband focused on product development and marketing.

Following her husband's death, Anna managed to raise four children by herself and braved the challenge of leading a million-dollar company with unmatched leadership skills and brilliant entrepreneurial instincts.

Upon her death in 1934, Anna Sutherland Bissell was applauded for being a "successful businesswoman in an era where business was almost wholly a masculine field". Anna is acclaimed as a brand strategist, top-notch sales expert, and ethical leader who made meaningful contributions to the Grand Rapids community.

"Two Tender Hearts"

Anna Sutherland was born on 2nd December 1846 in the picturesque little village of River John in Canada's Nova Scotia, to parents Eleanor and William. Eleanor Putnam was the daughter of renowned Canadian innovator, Charles Putnam, while William Sutherland served as a Scots Sea Captain. Anna was the youngest of her five siblings, adored and loved by all.

William was a seasoned sailor who would regale his children with riveting tales of his travels worldwide, feeding their imagination with animated stories of New Zealand's tree ferns, the breathtaking beauty of Cape Horn, and Australian harbors. Sadly, William's earnings as a sailor did not satisfy his desire to ensure his children grow up highly educated with great prospects to build gratifying lives.

Business prospects were few and far between in their quaint little village and across the whole of Nova Scotia's remote community. William set his sights on establishing a farm and relocated his family to Wisconsin, renowned as America's most fertile and innovative agricultural district.

In 1851, like innumerable settler families from England and France, the Sutherlands settled in De Pere, Wisconsin, and started running a farm. De Pere was a close-knit and welcoming community, and the kids began attending the local school.

Anna loved school and had an unquenchable thirst for learning. The fire of ambition and hard work burned bright and fierce in her heart from a very young age, and Anna dedicated herself to excelling at school to excel at life. She had mapped her journey well, and after graduating high school, 16-year-old Anna immediately started working as a teacher. However, unlike most female teachers, Anna's school was unconventional; she would teach underprivileged students out of an oxcart!

Three years later, she met a handsome young porcelain merchant, Melville Bissel, who was visiting De Pere. The two fell madly in love, tying the knot just three days before Anna's 19th birthday. Melville was a porcelain trader and a brilliant inventor, working in his family crockery business with his father, Alpheus, and brother, Harvey.

After their marriage, the couple moved to Kalamazoo and began their happily-married life. A letter from Melville's sister, published in *Recollections of Anna Bissell McCay*, offers insight into the couple's exemplary bond and love for each other.

Mary Bissell writes:

Melville and Anna always presented a picture in my mind of ideal lovers; their devotion, their unselfish thoughtfulness of one another's feelings and interests, their tender expression of the almost 'Divine love' given to two tender hearts makes me believe in the beautiful reality of the joys of wedded bliss, that the practical life has great possibilities of presenting a heavenly side to it, to those who are willing to think of others more than themselves – truly such lives are a part of the loving, compassionate Omnipotent Father, who loveth with a love beyond understanding....

Melville applauded Anna's intellect and entrepreneurial savviness, while Anna was her husband's loudest promoter, praising his inventions and promoting his fare to anyone who listened. She got creatively involved in the family business soon after the marriage, helping her husband manage the promotion and sales of the store's precious chinaware, crockery, and porcelain.

The couple welcomed five children to the world: Anna Dotelle, Melville Reuben, Harvey, Irving Joy, and Lillie May. Eager to expand his business and explore developed new markets for his inventions, Melville moved his family to Michigan's Grand Rapids. Little did they know that greatness and glory awaited their arrival in America's Furniture City!

The Right Way to Sweep!

In 1871, Anna and Melville moved to Grand Rapids and reopened their crockery store, Bissel & Sons, at 27 Canal Street. Anna was deeply involved in running the new business and introducing the store's fine china and porcelain pieces to the women in her community. Anna oversaw every aspect of the packaging and distribution, and as the inventory boxes packed with sawdust and straw would travel in and out of the house and office, they would leave storms of dust and debris on the carpets.

Anna helped unpack and place the merchandise to make the store aesthetically appealing to female customers. But unpacking was an uphill task, because the sawdust and straws would scatter around, pooling up in the carpet fibers. The Bissells, like other families in their neighborhood, owned a mechanical carpet sweeper. Still, it simply wasn't effective enough, compelling Anna to weed out the straws and beat out the dust herself.

Overwhelmed by the demanding chores of cleaning the dust-ridden carpets, Anna complained to her husband, and the ever-attentive and inventive Melville got to work immediately. It is essential to understand that back in the late 19th century, housework was physically strenuous and time-consuming, demanding women dedicated a significant chunk of their time to keeping their floors squeaky clean and dust-free.

This was a time when electricity and vacuum cleaners were unheard of, and most mechanical carpet sweepers on the market caused vast clouds of dust, creating more debris than they cleaned. As houses grew bigger and interiors became heavily adorned with furnishings and ornaments, carpeting emerged as a popular home décor trend to preserve wooden floors and maintain a tidy home.

Fully-carpeted floors were *a la mode* across America's upper- and middle-class families during the late 19th century, but the advent of carpets exacerbated cleaning challenges, demanding more effort and time than bare floors.

Women used brooms to beat out the dirt and dust, but brooms were highly ineffective and would spread out the dust more evenly than taking it out. This prompted women to seek more effective, deep cleaning rituals that involved a lengthy process of removing the carpet, taking it outdoors, beating out the dust with a carpet beater, and finally, reinstalling it.

Mechanical carpet sweepers took the American market by storm in the mid-19th century, operating a rotary brush on a motor connected to a pair of wheels. Women only had to push the sweeper, and the brush would rotate on its own, sweeping up the dirt and depositing it into a removable container that could be lifted and emptied easily.

These carpet sweepers were undoubtedly more effective and easier to handle than manual cleaning rituals. Still, they weren't an ideal solution, because of the huge dust clouds they left behind, making breathing hard. Melville decided to innovate the existing design with an efficient model that didn't emit dust and worked smoothly on even and uneven surfaces.

On September 19th, 1876, Melville invented the world-famous Bissell Carpet Sweeper, propelling Bissell & Sons toward global recognition. Even Queen Victoria instructed her staff to ensure the palace carpets were nicely "bisselled"!

The Making of a Leader Extraordinaire

Initially, Melville had no intention of producing and selling his carpet sweeper, because it was an invention he had engineered for his wife's ease and comfort. But the response his carpet sweeper garnered compelled him to change his mind. Customers visiting the store to shop for expensive china would notice the efficient device used on its carpets and inquire about its availability and price.

Everyone wanted to bring home the remarkable Bissell carpet sweeper, and Anna, well aware of the device's functionality and marketability, took charge of the product's branding and sales. After securing the patent for his ingenious innovation, the store began producing the Bissell carpet sweeper in the expansive manufacturing unit on the second floor.

Anna's astute business acumen and crafty sales techniques made the product an overnight sensation. She knew the carpet sweeper worked wonders at lightening the workload for homemakers and promoted its ability to eliminate the drudgery of carpet cleaning with masterful aplomb. Anna was appointed as head salesperson for the carpet sweeper, with a decisive role in production, marketing, and distribution.

From the beginning, Anna wanted to advertise the sweeper aggressively, reaching out to the local and nationwide audience with a multitude of mediums. She coined the popular catchphrase, "I prize my Bissell Sweeper", for the earliest advertisements and posters, turning Bissell Sweepers into a highly-coveted household product for American housewives. She managed to sell the first sweeper for $1.50.

Anna's mounting job responsibilities demand extensive travel to nearby cities, towns, and villages, promoting the new carpet sweeper with demonstrations and negotiating with local retailers. Anna and Melville hit the road soon after the sweepers turned out to be a massive hit in the Grand Rapids community, embarking on a door-to-door sales campaign.

The most enriching aspect that made Anna's advertising and sales strategies highly effective was her comprehensive knowledge of her product and its major selling points. She understood the burdens of maintaining a spotlessly clean home and used women's pain points to market her product's undeniable utility. She was an excellent demonstrator and would assemble and disassemble the carpet sweeper within seconds. Anna would handle the product demonstrations herself, traveling far and wide to demonstrate the sweeper's utility to hundreds and thousands of customers.

One fine day, according to the family's accounts narrated by the couple's daughter Anna Bissell McKay, Melville and Anna decided to target two streets in a busy commercial district in

Philadelphia. Philadelphia ranked among America's most dynamic marketplaces at the time, with hundreds and thousands of high-paying customers.

Anna approached the new, upmarket Wanamaker's, one of America's earliest department stores. Melville went in the opposite direction, armed with the Bissell Carpet Sweeper and their sales pitch. When the couple met a while later, Melville was delighted to discover that Anna had managed to sell her sample and taken orders for more than a dozen sweepers.

That's not all. The very same day, Anna had persuaded Wanamaker's to stock the Bissell Carpet Sweeper after wowing the owners with her creative sales pitch and detailed understanding of her product's uniqueness.

Anna's extensive, countrywide sales tours and deepening involvement in the production and distribution processes enriched her creative talents with real-world exposure to the male-dominated business realm. She polished her advertising acumen through customer interactions, honing her craft to excel at customer care with gracious after-sales services.

Overseeing the manufacturing, packaging, and distribution processes facilitated a keen sense of operational management in her and steered the workforce toward higher motivation and productivity. Anna was absorbing and learning as much as she could about corporate expansion and financial management, and all this knowledge was critical for the most challenging test of her entrepreneurial acumen, which was yet to come.

Highlighting her mother's commitment and dedication to the company, Anna Bissell McKay writes in her book:

She was always interested in her husband's activities and studied his business as many women study French. She took no small part in the early development of the business, traveled extensively in the company's interest, and secured the first order John Wanamaker (department store) of Philadelphia ever gave for carpet sweepers. There was no detail of the business with which she was not familiar.

A Disheartening Setback

During the 1880s, Bissell emerged as a household name worldwide, with housewives and their maids proudly demonstrating how they had "bisselled" their carpets to perfection! Anna's creative branding made the carpet sweeper a global symbol of perfect housekeeping and a must-have for Western domestic goddesses.

By now, American homemakers across the country's upper and middle classes couldn't do their daily cleaning without the Bissell Carpet Sweeper sharing their workload. Even Queen Victoria of England swore by the sweeper's utility and had her palace staff ensure all the carpets were nicely "bisselled" using the ingenious American invention.

The success of the sweepers was so phenomenal that Anna and Melville abandoned their crockery business entirely to focus solely on their best-selling invention. The couple continued expanding their company and, in 1882, constructed a larger factory to fulfill global demand by producing sweepers on a massive scale.

Just as profits started to soar in 1884, Anna and Melville were left reeling by a devastating fire that erupted in the factory, destroying everything in its wake. The couple's daughter, Anna Bissell McKay, recalls the harrowing details in her memoir:

The fire spread with lightning-like rapidity throughout the building and to a sawmill next door; thence to several adjoining factories, and all were completely destroyed. The loss to the Bissell Company was about sixty thousand dollars, and ninety men were out of employment. That very day, however, Melville R. Bissell declared that though his personal loss amounted to fifty thousand dollars, nevertheless he had 'good health, Western grit, and Christian fortitude' and he could make good.

The devastation of the factory was a massive blow for Anna and Melville, who had invested everything they had in expanding the production, putting all their eggs in one basket after shutting down their crockery line. The financial burdens triggered by this loss were crippling, but a determined Anna was ready to face and overcome this disheartening setback.

According to their daughter's account, Melville approached Grand Rapids' banking community for a loan to rebuild the factory. At the same time, Anna visited the merchants and vendors to return some of the costly raw materials the company had recently purchased. The vendors, impressed by the couple's credibility and integrity, insisted Anna keep the merchandise and pay for it later when she could.

Anna and Melville continued meeting with affluent bankers and businesspeople from Grand Rapids' burgeoning corporate community, swaying them with favorable profitability forecasts and the company's glowing references from retailers and suppliers. With her shrewd financial skills and crafty sales pitch, Anna secured a sizable bank loan covering the entire cost of repairing the fire-ravaged factory and its inventory!

This was a remarkable feat, and within a year, the couple had managed to rebuild the plant. Anna and Melville decided to mark the fire anniversary with a lavish feast for all employees in the new four-story brick building. In 1886, the Bissell Company was back in action, employing over 165 workers and selling Bissell Carpet Sweepers to tens of thousands of customers across America, Canada, and Europe.

Speaking of the couple's struggles from the time, Anna Bissell McKay writes that her mother's tireless efforts did "help father's standing wonderfully. She was a true helpmate if there ever was one."

When Tragedy Strikes

Five years after restarting the company, Melville developed pneumonia and became severely ill at the age of 45. Just four days later, on 5th March 1889, he passed away, leaving Anna and their children overwhelmed with grief and loss. Anna's daughter wrote of her mother's sadness, "The death of my father was the crowning tragedy of Mother's life".

Anna's heart was shattered upon losing the love of her life, but the newly-widowed mother of five was thrust into a new role: Chief Operating Officer of Bissell. Anna didn't get enough time to mourn her husband and lover, for she had to step up and fill Melville's empty chair and steer the fast-growing company toward profitability. Through sheer tragedy and unprecedented loss, Anna emerged as America's first female CEO.

Anna couldn't set aside her woes to mourn her husband, for she had to secure the future of her family and the company, demanding a course correction with bold steps. The Bissell family had mortgaged their property and home to secure the loan for the factory reconstruction. Anna took over the company's presidency in 1889 and successfully expanded the business throughout North America and Europe.

The first initiative Anna took after taking the reins as CEO was securing patents and trademarks to deter manufacturers and retailers from counterfeiting the Bissell Carpet Sweepers. She established a dedicated marketing department, using her experience as a brand and sales strategist to create a standardized system of advertising guidelines.

Anna poured her pain and sorrow into her work, and within ten years under her leadership, Bissell emerged as the world's largest manufacturer of carpet sweepers. When the 1890s arrived, Bissell was manufacturing and distributing over 1000 carpet sweepers daily. Anna opened a company branch in New York City, with factories producing and distributing the product in London, Paris, and Toronto. She also established a distribution and marketing network with agencies operating in over 20 countries.

Anna Bissell was a liberal employer with a reformist mindset who sought to reform human resource management and customer service practices by invoking a sense of community with family-oriented values. She was among America's first business leaders to focus on employee security with worker's compensation and pension plans.

She introduced fixed work hours, encouraging employees to avoid working outside their schedule. Anna was one of the first business leaders to introduce the novel concept of annual leave and restitution payments for employees injured on duty.

Anna Bissell dreamt of global success for Bissell, and she thrust the company into foreign markets with localized advertising, making the sweepers increasingly popular with women across America and Europe. In 1919, Anna was appointed President of the company's board, and she used this position to modernize the organization.

Anna infused everything she did with a personal touch, and her concern made her a revered mother figure for her employees. Her entrepreneurial acumen and shrewd business-mindedness transformed the company into a global trailblazer, sweeping its way toward a sizable domestic and foreign market share.

Today, Bissell Inc. is a testimony to Anna's creativity, entrepreneurial vision, and determination, thriving as a private family-owned-and-operated company with an extensive range of household products.

Inspiring Matriarch with a Heart of Gold

Anna is remembered for dreaming big and taking calculated risks to actualize her dream into practical realities. Melville and

Anna had a dream, which they could have ignored to enjoy the safety net created by their thriving crockery and porcelain business.

But their collective dream and vision ignited a fire in their hearts, compelling them to venture outside their comfort zones and hit the road for door-to-door campaigns, ready to assemble and disassemble the product with a crafty sales pitch emphasizing the sweeper's utility. It didn't take long for the Bissell Carpet Sweeper to become a household essential, as homemakers worldwide "bisselled" their carpets and rugs to maintain squeaky-clean homes.

Anna kept the dream alive long after Melville departed, pouring all her love and pain into the business she had established alongside her beloved husband and best friend. Early on, after losing Melville, Anna discovered that the best way to cope with her grief was by uplifting the less fortunate and sharing her bounties with the less privileged. Anna was a gracious philanthropist intensely occupied with numerous civic engagements while managing a company and raising five children.

Anna served on the board of Blodgett Home for Children and facilitated healthcare access with her contributions at the Union Benevolent Assn (now serving the Grand Rapids community as the Blodgett Memorial Medical Center). She was a board member of the Clark Memorial Home and the only female National Hardware Men's Association member.

Her family and friends would lovingly call her "Saint Ann", applauding her numerous philanthropic initiatives despite her exhausting domestic and work responsibilities. According to her daughter's accounts, Anna never neglected her children, household duties, friendships, or even her love for reading. Somehow, she managed to run a multimillion-dollar company, help her community and be there for her kids every day without faltering.

Speaking to a journalist about her civic contributions, Anna once said, "I believe the only way to make the world better is by personal contact with those who need to be helped."

The Bissell House, a community and recreation center for underprivileged immigrants and the Grand Rapids youth, had a special place in Anna's heart. The Bissell House was established in 1897, featuring a public library, a nursery, a playground, a gymnasium, a kindergarten, and recreational spaces. The upper level featured numerous apartments for the facility's managers and employees.

Anna had envisioned the Bissell House as a community hub of social connectivity and a support system for young working mothers and the youth. The facility offered many classes for boys and girls, including business studies, cooking, dancing, gardening, literature, and sports. Bissell House also provided a public bath, and there was always a long line for children and their mothers awaiting their turn to bathe.

Anna Bissell was an optimist, passionate about uplifting others and changing the world. In an interview published in the Grand Rapids Herald in 1930, an 84-year-old Anna shared her philosophy: "The world has always been nice to me. There is only one thing I would change if I could live it all over again. I would do 14 times as much for others. So much has been given to me."

During the 1930s, Anna moved with the rapidly-evolving pace of mechanics and innovated the Bissell Carpet Sweeper to maintain its competitiveness in a world obsessed with noise-free vacuum cleaners. When she passed away in 1934, the local newspapers remembered her as a "business executive without peer, a respected and beloved philanthropist, and a true matriarch in her family."

Tributes began to pour in from all over the world to commemorate Anna Bissel's legacy and contributions. Still, the most heartfelt tribute was a plaque Anna's employees presented to the Bissell family. The plaque read:

In memory of Mrs. M.R. Bissell, Sr., whose beautiful life combined business sagacity and American patriotism with faith in God and love of humanity. Her memory is enshrined in the hearts of her employees, by whom this tablet is erected. The world is better that she lived.

Having outlived her beloved Melville by 45 years, Anna remained the chair of the Bissell Company Board till her death on 8th November 1934. She was buried in Michigan's Oakhill Cemetery. In 1989, Anna was included in the Michigan Women's Hall of Fame, revered as America's first female CEO.

In 2016, the Grand Rapids community honored Anna Bissell's memory with a 7-foot bronze sculpture of her, on the spot where Anna and Melville established their first factory in the 1800s.

Anna Bissell's inspiring life and legacy are best summed up in her daughter's words, published in her book:

Trusting her own judgment even in the face of discouragement, she had great self-reliance, believed in enterprise, and had faith in her own resources; and so ends on this high note a beautiful life such as is given to few women to enjoy; or to pass on to her descendants a legacy so rich in example, in memories so happy, or in inspiration so great.

Chapter 2.6: Hattie Carnegie (1889-1956)

"We have the loveliest women in the world in this country, and wherever there are beautiful women, there will be beautiful clothes. To show the American woman herself off to best advantage - that has always been my aim, and that is my real biography."

— Hattie Carnegie

Armed with avant-garde cuts and fashionable styles, a sharply-tailored knee-grazing suit, and a look that radiated Parisian elegance, Hattie Carnegie broke free from the shackles of poverty. She rose to become the sole owner of a $6,500,000-worth fashion brand.

Hattie Carnegie rose to fame as a forward-looking style connoisseur at a time when fashion wasn't just a business, it was a revered form of fine art. In the roaring 40s, glamor was an art, and Hattie Carnegie was an artist extraordinaire, crafting every piece with matchless finesse and keen attention to detail.

Hattie's designs were way ahead of her time, introducing modern American women to various styles that liberated their curves and accentuated their forms with glamorous aplomb. Hattie Carnegie made fashion affordable for the woman on the street, filling the racks of local boutiques and departmental stores with cheap renditions of European and Parisian haute couture.

Hattie was her own most glamorous muse, rocking her boldly-structured suits and elegant dresses on her brisk, petite, sensual figure. No other designer could compete with her boundless knowledge of European fashion and operational awareness of running a profitable fashion business. During the early 1930s, Hattie Carnegie was America's most sought-after connoisseur of Parisian style, adapting European haute couture to American aesthetics with an affordable line of ready-to-wear dresses and suits.

She was the first designer to demonstrate that haute couture can be affordable and accessible for middle-class and working-class women, dressing them in finely-crafted designs that inspired confidence and elegance. During the war, Hattie overcame governmental restrictions on fabric use, and despite being cut off from the fashion Mecca of Paris, she managed to create the iconic "Carnegie look".

Carnegie is credited with exploring new dimensions and creating an exclusive, Americanized look that allowed American women to look past Parisian fashion and discover new cuts and styles to flaunt their curves. The Carnegie look embodied Hattie's ideals of an elegant and well-dressed woman – an attractive femme with a gay attitude and nifty dressing!

The iconic Carnegie suit is enshrined in fashion history with as much aplomb as the little black dress. Interestingly, Hattie was one of the first fashion aficionados to dispel the myths around age-appropriate dressing, encouraging women to dismiss the age factor while picking out cute outfits. Hattie Carnegie is quoted to have said, "It's much better to wear clothes that are too young for you than clothes which are too old!"

Hattie's philosophy was grounded in the feminist values of agency, autonomy, and independence – especially independence from the male gaze. Through her stylishly-structured suits and dresses, Hattie wanted women to command attention the moment they stepped inside a room, compelling people to applaud, "What a beautiful woman!" instead of saying, "What a beautiful dress!"

A Jewish Immigrant in New York City

Hattie Carnegie was born Henrietta Kanengeiser on 15th March 1886 in Vienna, Austria. Her father, Isaac Kanengeiser, was a tailor specializing in women's clothing. Tailoring in the late 19th century was regarded as an artisanal craft. Isaac was a true artist, well-versed in selecting delicate fabrics and designing finely-tailored clothing.

Legend has it that despite living in extreme poverty, Isaac gave his daughter Henrietta a love for designing and dressing up, inspiring her to drape her petite form with elegantly-styled attire. Henrietta was the second among seven siblings and enjoyed a warm bond of friendship with her father.

Many historians and journalists believe that Isaac introduced his daughter Hattie to the glamorous fashion world. In 1900, the Kanengeiser family relocated to America after a fire destroyed their house in Vienna, forcing them to find a new home.

Prospects were slim in 20th century Vienna, and hundreds of Austrian and German Jewish families were immigrating to the United States to find lucrative opportunities and achieve the big American dream. Hattie's family settled in New York City's Lower East Side, where she attended the local public school alongside her siblings.

Isaac, a seasoned and talented tailor and designer, found employment in New York City's thriving garment marketplace. Hattie often accompanied her father to work, absorbing and learning much about the city's garment and fashion industry. Isaac encouraged Henrietta to develop a skillset and become a modern working woman. Still, like most old-fashioned Jewish parents from that period, he also wanted to see her happily married.

For her parents, Henrietta's marriage meant a secure future for their daughter, and there was little concept of a love marriage at the time. Her parents had found love and companionship through an arranged match and envisioned the same for their daughter. So, Isaac found a good match in Ferdinand Fleischman, an Austrian American whose family had moved to America around the same time as Hattie's family.

Hattie's father fixed the match, but she married Ferdinand years down the line. Multiple sources maintain that as a teenager, Hattie fell madly in love with John Zanft, a Jewish American serving in the US military, who later became her second husband. Hattie's parents did not consider John a good match, because he was American, and they feared Hattie would lose her love for her Austrian culture and traditions.

Before he could marry his beloved daughter to his chosen beau, Ferdinand, Isaac fell ill, and a 13-year-old Hattie had to quit school to help support her family financially. She found a job at the Macy's department store, starting her career as a milliner, like most iconic designers of her time. Isaac felt guilty about forcing Hattie into the workforce when she should be secure in a happy marriage, but Hattie was right where she needed and wanted to be: in the glamorous world of the Upper East Side.

Sadly, Hattie's father passed away before he could witness his talented daughter becoming America's most sought-after and talented fashion designer.

Henrietta Kanengeiser becomes Hattie Carnegie

Hattie's journey at Macy's began as a messenger, later promoted to an assistant in the millinery workroom, and finally trained as a milliner. In her free time, Hattie tapped into her inner creativity and designed exquisite hats, which she sold to women in her neighborhood. As her skill as a milliner improved, Hattie bid goodbye to Macy's and found a job in a millinery workroom, where she worked as a millinery model and trimmed hats.

The story of how Henrietta Kanengeiser became Hattie Carnegie is interesting, laced with the ambitions, dreams, and passions that guided Hattie's transformation from a timid Austrian girl to a bold, innovative, and vivacious young woman seeking prosperity and opportunities in America.

Legend has it that Henrietta had once asked who America's most successful and wealthiest person was. Someone had replied, "Andrew Carnegie". That response stuck with Henrietta for years, resonating with her substantial fame, prosperity, and success aspirations.

When she turned 20, her experiences in the NYC fashion industry and elite society gave birth to the desire to reinvent her image, especially her name. So, Henrietta took "Carnegie" from Andrew Carnegie, perhaps after a premonition that this surname would bring her good luck and triumph. And to give her name a posh, aristocratic edge, she turned Henrietta into "Hattie". And thus, Hattie Carnegie was born!

During this time, Hattie worked at a wholesale dress shop, a job that did not require designing or sewing skills but which demanded a keen sense of fashion, style, and selling. Hattie had never educated herself in cutting, sewing, or sketching, but her sense of style was extraordinary. It didn't take long for the boutique's owner to notice her ability to sway customers by layering the right pieces and creating elegant outfits.

Hattie oversaw the dress ensembles, and the outfits she designed sold like hotcakes. Even though her styling talents garnered the shop a multitude of clients who wanted to be well-dressed, Hattie did not have much money to splurge on clothing. Recalling her minimal wardrobe from that period, she once said, "I had one skirt and three blouses for ages."

Her limited wardrobe certainly did not stop Hattie from flaunting her impeccable and sensational sense of style, drawing attention everywhere she went. Hattie Carnegie was a woman who made people stop in their tracks, compelled to turn and admire her elegantly-styled outfit, voluminous blonde hair, and bright blue eyes. She had a sophisticated aura, and her creatively-styled looks gave her a perfectly polished and primed appeal, much like the upper-class women she catered to at the store.

Using her discerning aesthetic sense and crafty styling talents, Hattie fashioned herself into an avant-garde and modern arbiter of fashion and glamor, attracting wealthy elite patrons like Mrs. William Randolph Hearst and Tallulah Bankhead, who trusted Hattie to dress them up for prestigious galas and privileged engagements.

When she turned 22, loyal to her father's wishes, Hattie tied the knot with Ferdinand Fleischman, hoping she could find love in an arranged marriage despite her undying love for John Zanft. The marriage was sour, and Hattie found solace in pursuing her core passion and the opera, which was a much-loved outlet for all the spare change she could save. She once told a journalist about her love for the opera, "I must have seen Madam Butterfly at least 50 times!"

A Budding Fashion Connoisseur

Hattie Carnegie was a style sensation in her neighborhood, flaunting the latest trends with elaborately-trimmed hats and her creations, trailing the streets like a queen adorned with elegant frills and tasteful colors. Women were quick to embrace whichever style or trend Hattie wore, mimicking how she styled her hair and layered her clothing into impeccably-styled outfits.

It didn't take long for Hattie to catch the eye of Rose Roth, a famous seamstress catering to women in the neighborhood. Rose saw Hattie as a walking clothing advertisement, attracting women with her undeniable poise and style savviness, tempting them to flaunt their curves with a similar attitude and style.

Rose Roth approached Hattie with a proposition, offering clothing for Hattie to flaunt if she could send women who inquire about her attire to shop at her store. Hattie agreed, and the two started a lucrative partnership, but soon, the potential for more growth and quadrupled profits materialized into a joint business venture.

In 1909, Hattie Carnegie and Rose Roth became partners. They opened a dressmaking and millinery boutique on NYC's East 10th Street, naming it Roth-Carnegie Inc. Hattie had little knowledge of designing or cutting clothes, let alone sewing them. She happily left these trivial matters to her more experienced and skilled partner, focusing on amassing a posh clientele of New York's wealthy socialites and privileged aristocratic women.

Her innate aesthetic talents and discerning eye for styles and trends bestowed the newly-opened boutique with affluent patronage, including Wallace Simpson, who later became the Duchess of Windsor, Mrs. WK Vanderbilt, and Mrs. William Randolph Hearst. Such was the spell of Hattie's phenomenal fashion sense that these well-heeled patrons would trust her judgment on everything, from undergarments and accessories to daywear and haute couture.

The business venture was a roaring success, even though Hattie and Rose never paid a single dime to advertise their designs in local magazines, as was the norm back then. Hattie found promoting uncouth and vulgar and believed street style was the most effective strategy to attract new customers and continue tempting their existing clientele.

In true New Yorker fashion, Hattie Carnegie would hit the streets dressed to the nines in the boutique's trendiest designs, modeling the latest outfits at social events and fine dining establishments. Hattie became a highly-regarded style connoisseur of New York City's elite society, flaunting Rose's recent creations at prestigious balls and charity events to attract their target clientele.

Amazingly, New York's dainty debutantes, fashionable patricians, and stylish socialites had to have everything they saw Hattie flaunting about town, from hats and gloves to dresses and skirts. The prices at the store started from around $75, which was quite outrageously expensive for the early 20th century. Still, the shrewd ladies targeted America's wealthy elite, who could undoubtedly spare the money to adorn themselves in the season's finest fabrics and frills.

Interestingly, despite passionately working in a fiercely competitive industry that appreciates and rewards talent, Hattie Carnegie never felt the need to learn how to sew. Hattie didn't need to learn sewing or knitting, because she had a far more precious and unique talent: the ability to guide sewers in designing form-flattering clothes and high-fashion attire that appealed to women's tastes.

By 1913, Roth-Carnegie Inc. was enjoying exponential success, prompting the two partners to relocate to NYC's fashionable quarters with a more expansive venue on West 86th Street.

Hattie Carnegie Inc. Is Born

In 1918, Hattie bought out Rose Roth's share in the business, ending their partnership over creative differences. Hattie wanted to steer the company in a different direction, and later that year, she opened a custom dressmaking business, a grand salon named "Hattie Carnegie Inc."

The salon was expansive and exceptionally well-appointed – an urbane setting to attract affluent and wealthy patrons interested in exclusive dresses and outfits tailored to their form. Hattie hired talented designers, sewers, and tailors, instructing them on the cuts, drapes, and styles she wanted to introduce under her label.

During this period, Hattie Carnegie mentored and tutored some of the brightest, most talented designers, who would become globally recognized, including Claire McCardell, Muriel King, Norman Norell, and Travis Banton.

In 1919, Hattie embarked on her first buying trip to Paris. It was common for American designers in the early 20th century to tour the Parisian markets and return home with the latest creations designed by European maestros. America's popular fashion boutiques, like Bergdorf Goodman and Carnegie's, would attend the Parisian fashion shows, buy dresses in bulk and sell them under their original labels or adapt them to American aesthetics and sell replicas to their wealthy clientele.

Back then, it was believed that high fashion originated in Paris, and Hattie would plan as many as seven trips to France a year, maintaining an apartment in Paris. During the height of her success, Hattie Carnegie bought over 70 dresses from every collection. Hattie Carnegie Inc. sold everything from Chanel and Gucci originals to Hattie's interpretation of the designs created by the grand fashion maestros.

Hattie's tours to Paris facilitated a dynamic learning experience. She would attend fashion shows and exhibits featuring the styles of high-end Parisian designers, learning everything she could about European high fashion and exquisite materials used to design glamorous haute couture pieces. Upon her return to America, Hattie poured all her newly-acquired knowledge and inspiration into curating avant-garde collections featuring classy French designs and the finest fabrics manufactured across America.

Hattie Carnegie established a thriving fashion empire through extraordinary creativity, futuristic innovation, and tireless hard work, selling custom-made designs at her salon and wholesaling affordable, ready-to-wear lines under the Hattie Carnegie Originals label. By this time, leading department stores across America, including Neiman Marcus and I. Magnin, were stocking her designs.

Hattie's exponential success from this period is partly accredited to her sound business acumen in setting up manufacturing units to manufacture her ready-to-wear lines. She owned multiple factories and was known to be highly involved, touring the factory floors, inspecting the clothing, and tweaking designs by adding a button or two or raising the hemline by an inch.

1928 was a splendid year for Hattie Carnegie. After divorcing Ferdinand, she tied the knot with her long-time flame, Major John Zanft. Hattie was a glamor sensation by this time, well-known throughout the United States and Paris. John willingly accepted living in the enormous shadow of this well-connected social butterfly.

John loved Hattie, and instead of resenting her success and popularity, he encouraged Hattie to continue expanding her company beyond clothing, branching out to include accessories, fine jewels, and clothing lines targeting children and males. Despite assisting her with multiple operational aspects of running the business, John never claimed any credit for her success. But Hattie never failed to shower him with praise, proudly declaring her love for her husband in interviews and publicly.

Until 1928, Hattie's business was thriving on custom-made attire and dresses, but she wanted to offer something affordable and effortless to the modern American femme. She introduced her first ready-to-wear collection, hiring designer Norman Norell to design the entire line. Hattie's grand studio had transformed into a department store during this period.

The following year, businesses across America were reeling from the slowdown triggered by the 1929 Stock Market Crash, but Hattie's business churned out $3,500,000 worth of profits.

Initially, the economic turmoil did not affect her sales, but gradually, she realized that many of her previously cash-rich patrons could not clear their dues.

To retain her clientele and attract scores of new customers, Hattie decided to introduce a new line, Spectator Sports. Each design was sold at $40 each – still quite expensive for the early 20th century, but considerably more affordable than her custom-made dresses.

Soaring Heights of Success

Hattie's boutique on East 49th Street continued expanding. It quadrupled in size, becoming a retail paradise for shopaholics and style-savvy socialites looking to splurge their money on exquisite fur, custom-made designer attire, costume jewels, knitwear, perfumes, and accessories. By this time, Hattie was selling everything *a la mode*, from artisanal chocolate bonbons and coveted European antiques to sharply-tailored blouses, scents, scarves, and more.

She is credited with introducing American consumers to the "head-to-hem boutique" concept, starting a roaring trend that multiple successful designers, including Michael Kors and Ralph Lauren, adopted. Hattie Carnegie was a connoisseur and collector, and fashion experts remember her contributions to the industry as an editor instead of a designer.

Renowned American designer Geoffrey Beene once commented on Hattie's talents and boutique:

When I arrived in New York from my studies in Paris, I approached the house of Hattie Carnegie for first employment. I knew Mrs. Carnegie was not a designer but a great editor, and I had heard of her reputation for superb taste. I never worked for her—but if she were here now, I would still be trying!

It wouldn't be wrong to regard Hattie Carnegie as an editor, because instead of designing her collections, she curated by guiding her team of designers and seamstresses with her expert opinions on the reigning trends of New York City, Paris, Milan, and London. She is credited with introducing American women to iconic trends, many of which have become timeless classics that can never lose their glamorous appeal.

These trends include sparkles and sequins on festive dresses, knee-grazing hemlines and skirts, floor-length cocktail dresses, and the infectious chicness of capes. Hattie's most iconic and celebrated creation is the sharply-tailored and boldly-structured "Little Carnegie Suit".

Hattie Carnegie is also accredited for liberating the curves of American women from the ridiculously uncomfortable and unpleasant corsets that caused breathing constraints.

Legend has it that in 1939, Hattie wore a corset, a French invention, to test it out for her American customers. As it happened, Hattie had to catch a plane back to the US the same day and got unbearably uncomfortable mid-flight. So much so that she requested the stewardess and secretary to help her get out of the "living casket", declaring the corset unsuitable for her American patrons.

During this period, Hattie's fame was unparalleled, and the demand for her products was unprecedented. Celebrities and wealthy patrons pranced around in her shop day in and night out, buying everything she had found worthy of displaying in her retail haven. Interestingly, Hattie's brand is accredited for introducing some of Hollywood's most iconic celebrities as models, including Betty Davis, Sophia Loren, Joan Crawford, and Lucille Ball.

During the 1940s, she launched the Blue Room, Hattie Carnegie Perfumes, and Cosmetics Inc. and later introduced a line for children, the Jeune Fille.

Hattie visited Paris at least three to four times a year until World War Two arrived, halting her trips and access to European inspiration and materials. As French fabrics became a rarity in America, Hattie began seeking crafty new ways to present American women with form-flattering attire.

An Immigrant's Patriotic Duty

World War Two impacted the global fashion industry in more ways than one. Restrictions on fabric use and foreign trade denied designers the freedom to craft their artistic designs. In America, the US government introduced a series of restrictions with the L-85 ruling in 1942, limiting the dimensions of fabric yardage that could be used to manufacture every piece of clothing, from blouses and dresses to jackets and skirts.

Boutiques and designers on Seventh Avenue went into a frenzy over fabric shortages and yardage restrictions that didn't leave much room for creative expression. But the legendary Hattie Carnegie had a solution for every problem. Her iconic Carnegie Suit emerged as the perfect silhouette to flaunt a sharply-tailored look without needing extensive yards of fabric.

In 1950, the United States Army approached Hattie, NYC's resident impresario of custom-made attire, to reinvent her elegant Carnegie Suit for the Women's Army Corps. This project was incredibly special for Hattie, who remembered the teenage immigrant who had arrived in New York with big dreams, changing her surname to Carnegie in the home of actualizing America's essence of freedom and prosperity.

Interestingly, by this time, a 65-year-old Hattie had all but retired, and her focus was on spending quality time at home reconnecting with her husband, John, on their luxurious Four Winds Ranch. John was a US military veteran of World War I, and Hattie would lovingly call him "my American soldier".

She wasn't visiting the stores and factories as frequently as she had in the past, when she would stop by multiple times a week to share new designs with her designers, discuss new sketches or meet her clients. But when the US Military commissioned her to design the Women's Army Corps uniforms, Hattie enthusiastically went back to work, calling it the "proudest moment" of her life.

Hattie redesigned the WAC uniforms, modeling the design after her elegant Carnegie Suit and replacing the unflattering olive-green wool with a feminine rosy glow. Hattie's creation was splendid, balancing understated elegance with sleek and intelligent tailoring to emphasize the professionalism demanded by the armed forces.

She discarded the heavy army-issued cotton blouse, replacing it with feather-soft silk, and gave the caps a chic appeal by placing the insignia in the middle. Despite resistance from the senior leadership, Hattie insisted that the skirts should maintain a fashionable length slightly below the knee.

Considering the project to be a patriotic duty to the country that adopted her and helped her find the path to success, Hattie

Carnegie refused to accept any payment for redesigning the WAC uniforms. Despite dressing some of Hollywood's most iconic and highly-acclaimed actresses, including Joane Fontaine, Tallulah Bankhead, and Joan Crawford, redesigning the WAC uniforms was Hattie's favorite project.

The women of the WAC first wore the uniform on New Year's Day, 1951, and it remained in use till 1968. In 1952, Hattie Carnegie was awarded the Congressional Medal of Freedom for designing the Women's Army Corp uniform.

As fate would have it, Hattie's favorite project was her most significant and highly-acclaimed contribution to the fashion industry. The restrictions imposed under Ruling L-85 created challenges for businesses, designers, and retailers, resulting in unprecedented losses, and by designing the WAC uniform, Hattie had given the industry an ingenious low-cost solution, starting the low-grade fashion fever that consumed the global fashion sector throughout the war. Airlines began mimicking Hattie's WAC uniform, and the knee-grazing hemlines for dresses became *a la mode*.

Hattie's Love for Costume Jewelry

Hattie had a love for jewelry and precious stones, and she was a passionate collector. Her signature accessory was a delicate strand of oriental pearls, gifted by her beloved husband, John

Zanft. Like Coco Chanel, Hattie Carnegie wanted to create head-to-toe style statements adorned with accessories like costume jewelry and hats.

In 1955, she started expanding the vision and product lineup for Hattie Carnegie Costume Jewelry Inc., including jewelry pieces to pair with her clothing line, especially her iconic Carnegie Suits. This would be Hattie's final project, launched only a year before she passed away in 1956.

Hattie's jewelry was strikingly different from the conventional choice of attire and traditional ready-to-wear lines. Her venture into costume jewelry revealed Hattie's wilder side, her love for exotic oriental motifs, and her flair for playfulness. It appeared that her jewels were meant to spice up the conservative outfits she was selling, elevating the elegance with fun-filled glam.

Since she wasn't a designer herself, Hattie commissioned innumerable highly-talented jewelry designers, working with renowned artists such as Kenneth Jay Lane and notable French sculptor Nadine Effront. Hattie's jewelry pieces deviated from the same-old replicas of gemstones and fine jewelry, featuring a juxtaposed blend of multiple influences, from African and Asian art to East Indian exoticism and Egyptian Revival art.

Instead of working with fine metals, Hattie designed her pieces with enamels, gilt metals, and plastics. During the 1950s, Hattie made waves with her exquisite animal-shaped brooches, inspired by African art and carved with Lucite. She introduced a lineup of bold and vibrant pins in enigmatic shades like emerald green, ivory, turquoise blue, and red-orange, embellished with colorful beads and sparkly rhinestones.

The Carnegie jewels distinguished themselves from the pieces sold by other brands with their intricate detailing, creativity, and ingenious use of innovative materials. Hattie introduced bold and wild accessories that made her collection a staggering success in New York's roaring "cocktail jewelry" movement, for which women glammed up their outfits with flamboyant pieces like chunky earrings, heavy bracelets, and demi-parures of chokers, and necklaces.

Instead of churning out typical floral, fruity, or nature-themed designs, Hattie offered her clientele a variety of trendy materials, such as glass beads, artificial pearls, enamel, and crystal rocks. The Oriental Jewelry line was Hattie's most iconic and celebrated collection, fashioned after designs from Indian culture and the Far East. The exhibition featured animal and human figures crafted with rare metals and adorned with faux pearls and rhinestones.

After Hattie Carnegie passed away in 1956, the jewelry she designed just before her death became known as the brand's most precious pieces, with enormous value for collectors and vintage jewelry enthusiasts to this day.

The Woman Who Invented American Fashion

In 1948, Hattie Carnegie became the proud recipient of the Coty American Fashion Critics Award in recognition of her innovative and endlessly-vast contributions to the American fashion industry. Her unmatched knack for combining suitable fabrics, styles, and textures made her a sought-after connoisseur of custom-made attire, garnering her multiple commissions from revered institutions, including the US Army. Hattie Carnegie was also commissioned to design habits for the Carmelite Sisters, an order of the Society of the Church of Christ.

Hattie Carnegie's legacy stems from her wide-ranging impact on America's fashion history, alongside influencing trends across fashion capitals worldwide. The 1930s were a glorious period for female designers, allowing them to overshadow male stylists who had ruled the arena of women's clothing for far too long.

Hattie carved a unique fashion identity for American women by facilitating a departure from the shadows of Parisian fashion and European couture. She actively encouraged American women to cultivate their unique style identity by introducing trendy statements that would define the modern American woman and her penchant for functional elegance.

Fate did not allow her to pursue a formal education. Still, she dedicatedly educated herself throughout her life, gaining firsthand experience from her work and surrounding herself with innovative experts. She inspired women to break free from the stifling constraints of unflattering corsets, yards of unshapely fabric, and all the silhouettes that denied them the opportunity to take pride in their curvature and form.

As Hattie once said, "My clothes are built to show off the woman who wears them. I like them to be simple, complicated and simple, to move well, to move with the times and a little ahead of the times." A forward-thinking style aficionado, Hattie was a passionate supporter of the women's rights movement and a strong advocate for women's financial independence and empowerment through hard work and entrepreneurial ventures.

Conclusion

We often face challenges and roadblocks that dishearten and dissuade us from pursuing our ambitions and goals. These inspiring stories of relentlessly-determined and unyieldingly-persistent women demonstrate how hardships knead and hone our innate talents into highly-marketable skills that lead us toward success. From this perspective, challenges and struggles are the most crucial and instrumental ingredients for success, helping dreamers develop masterful leadership skills.

If you found these gripping tales of preservation, resilience, and success inspiring, you must follow the example set by these remarkable women. If they achieved prosperity and triumph at a time when all odds were pitted against women, you can most certainly fulfill your ambitions using the female-centric ecosystems established to facilitate business ownership for modern-day women.

We urge you to inspire us by emailing us about your experiences and entrepreneurial struggles at
EmiliaFine@greensleeves-publishing.com

Don't forget to leave a review at the link to the book page, and tell us which story inspired you the most!